La Bolshie Vita

A Comedy

Ken Whitmore

Suggested by *The Government Inspector* by Nikolai Gogol

Samuel French – London
New York – Sydney – Toronto – Hollywood

ISBN 0 573 01648 8

CHARACTERS

Sonya Alexandrovna, a servant girl, aged 22
Natasha Antonovna, her young mistress, 22
Militia Sergeant
Ivan Alexandrovich, a dissident poet, 30
Osip Constantinovich, hero project volunteer, 22
Anton Antonovich, Poshlost Party Secretary, 50
Anna Andreyevna, Anton's wife, 45
Bobchinsky
Dobchinsky
Colonel Bullbich
Girl

The parts of the Militia Sergeant and Colonel Bullbich may be doubled. The brief non-speaking part of the Real Commissar in the final scene may be played by a man or a woman.

LA BOLSHIE VITA

First presented at the Birmingham Repertory Theatre on
19th February, 1986, with the following cast:

Sonya Alexandrovna	Marie Francis
Natasha Antonovna	Allison Harding
Militia Sergeant	Paul Mulrennan
Colonel Bullbich	
Ivan Alexandrovich	Marc Culwick
Osip Constantinovich	Timothy Watson
Anton Antonovich Dmukhanovsky	Paul Kiernan
Anna Andreyevna	Devon Scott
Bobchinsky	Crispin Redman
Dobchinsky	Iain Glen

Directed by Derek Nicholls
Designed by Ian MacNeill

ACT I
   Scene 1   A platform on the Yaroslavsky station,
                Moscow
   Scene 2   A platform on Poshlost station, Siberia
   Scene 3   Anton's house
   Scene 4   A hillside near Poshlost
   Scene 5   Anton's house
   Scene 6   Poshlost market square

ACT II
   Scene 1   Anton's house
   Scene 2   Sonya's private plot
   Scene 3   Anton's house
   Scene 4   A birch glade

Time—the present

PRODUCTION NOTE

No trains appeared on the stage in the original production. They were suggested by sounds. New scenery was wheeled smartly on and off by the cast in view of the audience, to the accompaniment of current Soviet pop songs, and this facilitated a swift and fluid production lasting a little under two hours, not counting the interval.

ACT I*

A platform on the Yaroslavsky Station, Moscow. There is a bench, a statue of Lenin, the door to a refreshment buffet, a tall and complicated-looking Russian-language timetable, a trestle-table full of rubber stamps and the rest of the paraphernalia of passport control

Introductory music fades down and a railway announcement in Russian is heard in the distance

An armed Militia Sergeant comes to the trestle-table, checks through some documents on it, then stands examining passers-by with profound suspicion

Sonya, a girl of twenty-two, enters, carrying baggage for two. She is hurrying and calling to somebody behind

Sonya Oh, come on, Natasha! Stop dawdling! We're going to miss our train! Come on, come on, come on!

Natasha (*off*) All right, all right, all right!

Sonya Well hurry! Just look at the girl. Leaves me with all the luggage and still can't keep up. Forever in a dream. Wake up, Natasha! Hurry! Oh, how I hate railway stations. How I hate cities. Won't I be glad to put Moscow behind me and smell the fresh country air. Natasha! Do hurry!

Natasha enters

Natasha All right, Sonya. And don't yell at me. You're only a servant girl and I'm your mistress. Just remember your place.

Sonya My place is on the Red Arrow Express to Siberia and so is yours, Natasha Antonovna. We must find the right platform. If we got on the wrong train we could end up in Samarkand.

Natasha Samarkand! Oh, Sonya, what a wonderful mistake!

Sonya And keep your eyes open for Anton Antonovich and Anna Andreyevna.

Natasha I'll keep my eyes open but I won't see a thing. They're full of tears. Oh, Sonya Alexandrovna, I want to stay in Moscow for ever.

Sonya Yes and I want to put it behind me till my dying day. I only came here to buy a steel garden fork but there's a two-year waiting list.

Natasha Then let's wait! Oh, do let's, Sonya. Call me a taxi and we'll go straight back to Auntie Olga's.

---

*N.B. Paragraph 3 on page ii of this Acting Edition regarding photocopying and video-recording should be carefully read.

Sonya When our visitors' permits have expired? Are you mad? They'll throw us in prison.

Natasha But that's just where we're going—to the biggest, coldest prison of all—Siberia.

Sonya Siberia is home. Poshlost is home.

Natasha "Home can be the cruellest prison of all." Boris Pasternak.

Sonya You read too much.

Natasha And what else is there to do in Poshlost?

Sonya You could grow potatoes like me.

Natasha Yes, grow potatoes and marry that sadistic old KGB colonel Stepan Bullbich who terrorizes all Poshlost. Do you realize I promised him an answer when I returned from Moscow? But I thought I wouldn't *be* returning. I thought I'd find some dazzling diplomat . . . some astronaut . . . some poet . . . and put Siberia and Stepan Bullbich behind me for ever.

Sonya Well you found nobody so we must catch that train. In these shoes I don't fancy walking three thousand miles. Look, there's a militia man. He'll put us right.

Natasha Wait, Sonya.

Sonya Oh, what are you staring at now?

Natasha The Yaroslavsky Station. Did you know that Dr Zhivago set out from here?

Sonya What was it? A maternity case?

Natasha Oh, you're such a philistine. No, he was fleeing the turmoil of the civil war. Setting out for the Urals and the warm heaving breast of his beloved Lara.

Sonya Oh, bronchitis. Anyway, that book is banned so you mustn't talk about it. Now come on, Natasha.

Natasha No, wait! Can't you sense it?

Sonya Sense what?

Natasha The Yaroslavsky Station. It's full of ghosts. It was on this very spot that Count Vronsky fell in love with Anna Karenina as she stepped down from the train from St Petersburg.

Sonya Well we all know what happened to her.

Natasha Oh, yes, her life may have been tragic, but she lived, Sonya, she lived. She didn't merely exist. She never suffocated in a small Siberian town. If it hadn't been for the revolution I could have lived like Anna. My mother's family were aristocrats. That's why I dream of Moscow. It's in my blood.

Sonya Fine, so we'll go and ask the militia man where to catch the train.

Natasha Stop! That militia man looks just like Stepan Bullbich.

Sonya Yes, you can bet he's a KGB man. Come on. He won't bite.

Natasha (*going*) Don't be so sure.

Pause

Sonya Good-day to you, Comrade Sergeant.

Sergeant Good-day. All the better for your company, fair comrades.

Sonya Could you tell us where to catch the Trans-Siberian Express?

Sergeant This very platform, comrades. She's due in ten minutes. But wait. Don't tell me they're sending you beautiful maidens into exile.

Natasha Yes.

Sonya No.

Sergeant Yes-no?

Sonya We were born there.

Natasha Yes, for our sins, which must have been black as pitch. We've just had a week's holiday here with my Auntie Olga and now we're going back to prison.

Sonya Home.

Natasha Prison.

Sergeant And what have you been up to in Moscow? No, don't tell me. Let me guess. I'm not an ordinary policeman. I'm KGB.

Sonya Good heavens! Who'd have guessed?

Sergeant I'm posted here so I can keep an eye on everybody leaving or entering Moscow. Spies, wreckers, black marketeers, smugglers of ideologically harmful contraband. I can sum up people at a glance. Take you two. I'll tell you what you've been up to. You've been trying to hook husbands for yourselves.

Natasha What an appalling slander!

Sonya The very idea!

Sergeant No, you can't fool the KGB. The girls of this country outnumber the men by twenty millions because of all the purges and pogroms and wars. So the girls have to make all the running. And most of all they run after a Muscovite so they can get their paws on a Moscow residents' permit and live for ever in the people's paradise.

Natasha Why, I've never been so insulted in my life! Not even in Siberia! I'll have you know my father is an immensely high-up party official and he's coming home from the West today. Yes, the West! That's how high-up he is. And when he finds out you've been rude to me he'll box your big red ears. Come, Sonya! (*Going*) I need a glass of tea. This fellow's more of a bear than Stepan Bullbich, he really is . . .

Natasha and Sonya exit

Sergeant (*calling after them*) I say, why don't you get your big important daddy to buy you a husband at the market in Gorki Street? (*He laughs*)

Ivan enters. He is aged twenty-five, and has a rucksack on his back

Ivan Excuse me.

Sergeant Yes? What do you want?

Ivan I was told to report here and collect my ticket for Siberia.

Sergeant (*suspiciously*) Siberia? Oh, Siberia. Siberia, eh? Now which one are you then?

Ivan Which one am I?

Sergeant No, wait. Don't tell me. Let me guess. I happen to have two tickets for Siberia. This blue one here for a Jewish dissident satirical poet. And this red one here for a golden example of Soviet young manhood who's volunteered to work on a hero project building a gigantic new dam in the virgin lands.

Ivan Hero project?

Sergeant Thunder and damnation, I said let me guess! Why did you have to go and spoil it? But I had you spotted, comrade. You can't fool the KGB. A hero, I said, as soon as I saw the idealism shining in your face.

Ivan Amazing.

Sergeant It's just the way I was trained. Now then, did they tell you you'd be escorting a prisoner?

Ivan *I'll* be escorting a prisoner?

Sergeant Yes, the dissident scribbler.

Ivan Oy.

Sergeant And I've got orders to issue you with this. (*He produces a revolver*)

Ivan What? A revolver? But I've never——

Sergeant You were a crack shot in the Young Communists pistol team, according to this docket.

Ivan *I* was a crackshot?

Sergeant Damn it, I know you were! That's what I just said! (*He hands the revolver to Ivan*)

Ivan It won't go off, will it?

Sergeant Now if he gives you any trouble you know what to do. Bang.

Ivan I beg your pardon?

Sergeant Up against a wall. Bang.

Ivan *Gevalt!* What's he done?

Sergeant He's mentally ill and socially dangerous. He suffers from political delusions. He's written outspoken criticisms of the Soviet state. He's got an obsessive mania for truth-telling. And not only that—he wears a beard.

Ivan Well, there's nothing like a close shave.

Sergeant Quite right.

Ivan I've just had one.

Sergeant So I see. But listen, this joker had the nerve to apply for an exit visa to the West.

Ivan Oy! He sounds incorrigible.

Sergeant No, Lithuanian. And when they turned him down he offered a party boss a bribe of five hundred roubles.

Ivan But he wanted five thousand.

Sergeant Well, wheels don't turn without oil, you know. What did you say?

Ivan He wanted five thousand years.

Sergeant That's what he's getting.

Ivan He's what? But they said ... (*He pulls up short*)

Sergeant Yes?

Ivan Nothing.

Sergeant Little does he know it, but he's never coming back. He thinks he's being sent into internal exile, a cushy little number lifting spuds on a state farm, but there's a padded cell waiting for him.

Ivan No!

Sergeant Yes, he's off to a loony bin for lads with a deficient capacity for conforming to Soviet reality. They'll inject him with turpentine.

Ivan Oy!

Sergeant They'll wrap him up tight in a canvas sheet and run a watering can over him and when the canvas dries it'll shrink and the blood will gush from his nose and ears and in the end he won't have an unreliable thought in his head. (*Pause*) I wish I was coming with you, comrade.

Osip enters, looking lost. He consults the timetable

Ivan To the loony bin?

Sergeant To the hero project. You're a bit of a joker, aren't you? Yes, I wouldn't mind getting away from the wife for a spell. She's dead set on throwing the discus in the Olympic Games. Yes, she's had a course of these anabolic steroids.

Ivan Did they help?

Sergeant (*gloomily*) Yes, she's twice the woman she was. Look out, what's this lad want?

Osip Oh, good gracious, Sergeant.

Sergeant What?

Osip I mean good-afternoon. Evening? No, morning. That's to say how are you. I mean I am.

Sergeant Wait a minute. Wait a minute. Just slow down and start again.

Osip I was told to report here and tip out my pocket.

Sergeant Tip out your pocket?

Ivan You mean pick up your ticket?

Osip Thank you, comrade, yes, pick up my ticket.

Sergeant Oh, pick up your ticket. Pick up your ticket! Aha! So you're the blue one!

Osip Blue? No, I've never been happier.

Sergeant None of your sarcasm.

Osip Sarcasm? But I am happy. I'm off to Siberia, you see.

Sergeant Listen, you might have had a shave, my son, but you can't fool me.

Osip No, it's these bits of *Pravda* stuck on my face. They give the show away, don't they? I cut myself badly. It was my first shave.

Sergeant Yes, I know it was. I know all about your long beard.

Osip Pardon?

Sergeant Stop acting the clown. Do you think you're dealing with a moron? (*Aside*) Observe this man closely, comrade. Don't be fooled by his show of stupidity. It's all a big act. He's so plausible he once sold Bibles in the Kremlin. He tells more sob stories than Anton Chekhov. He's a bigger liar than the BBC. (*Aloud*) Now listen to me, Ivan Alexandrovich.

Osip Wait. My name's Osip.

Sergeant Lies! I've got it written down here on the blue ticket—Ivan Alexandrovich.

Osip Ah, but my name——

Sergeant Silence! Now listen, you're on your way to Siberia and you'll be

riding in the slave car. You'll be under constant surveillance by this young
fellow here and if there's any dirty work he's got orders to blow your
black brains to blue blazes.

Osip Hasn't there been some mistake? No, wait. Oh, yes, I get it. I get it.

Sergeant Yes, right between the eyes.

Osip Yes, that's very good. I see what you're up to now. It's a tough life I'm
going to and you're hardening me up, aren't you? Yes, Father warned me
it would be no Komsomol choir outing. To be honest, I thought he was
exaggerating. He didn't want me to go.

Sergeant Well, he wouldn't, would he?

Osip Nor Mother. Nor Tatiana.

Sergeant Who's Tatiana?

Osip My sister. Nor Bobik. He didn't want me to go either.

Sergeant Bobik?

Osip Father said, "They'll kill you. Stay at home. Work on the farm."
Mother said why does a nice boy with a university education want to run
off and play with a power drill on a hydro-electric dam when he can stay
at home and eat his fill of vegetables. Tatiana said who needs a dam when
you can get all the water you need from the tap.

Sergeant And what did Bobik say?

Osip Bobik? Are you serious? Bobik said nothing.

Sergeant Why not?

Osip Bobik's our wolfhound. I wanted to bring him with me but Mother
said it would be no life for a dog.

Sergeant She was right.

Osip That's when I got violent.

Sergeant Why, what did you do?

Osip I stuffed my vamp.

Sergeant You stuffed your vamp?

Osip Vamped my stuff.

Ivan Stamped your foot maybe?

Osip Yes, I stamped my foot right on Bobik's tail. He took a lump out of
my trousers. That's when I cut my ear. I was shaving at the time

*Anton and Anna enter, wheeling expensive luggage. They consult the
timetable*

Sergeant That's enough! My God, all this is pure invention. What did I tell
you, comrade? This is the sort of imagination we're up against. This man
has no family. They were all liquidated in the last Litvak purge. None of
these people exist. Except maybe the wolfhound. (*Pause*) But wait! Who
comes here?

Ivan Where?

Sergeant There. Over by Lenin's statue. I do believe it's a black marketeer
and his scarlet woman in white mink.

Ivan How on earth can you tell?

Sergeant What? Dressed like a duke? Chest puffed out as if he owns the
place? What else could he be?

Ivan A party official?

Sergeant You two push off. Go on. Off with you. That's right. Now. I'll nab this pair of beauties. (*Calling*) Oy! You! Rockefeller!

Anton (*distantly*) What? Me?

Sergeant Yes, you! Over here at the double!

Anton (*approaching*) All right, all right, enough of your shouting and bawling.

Sergeant Get fell in! Get fell in.

Anna Really! This is outrageous!

Sergeant Passports.

Anton I beg your——

Sergeant Passports! Turn out your pockets. Tip out your crocodile cases. Then strip to the buff.

Anna Oh! The saucy ruffian! Have you the slightest inkling of whom you might be undressing?

Sergeant Yes, one of the Mongolian Mafia and his overdressed trollop from the slums of Smolensk.

Anton By the bones of Saint Basil!

Sergeant Well and truly nabbed. A smuggler of ideologically harmful contraband and his tarted-up serf.

Anna A serf? I'll have you know, my friend, that I'm descended from the old nobility. My great aunt was the Grand Duchess Maria Merakovsky, a cousin of the Czar. Can't you see my Romanoff nose?

Sergeant Yes, roamin' off here, roamin' off there.

Anton Silence, you blockhead! Here. My passport. It will inform you that I am Anton Antonovich Skvoznik Dmukhanovsky, District Secretary of the Communist Party in Poshlost, Central Siberia, and Hero of Socialist Labour.

Sergeant Oh—ah—well—let me run and fetch you a glass of tea from the refreshment room.

Anton Silence! I've just built a tractor factory exactly on time in accordance with the five-year plan and that's why a grateful country rewarded me with its top decoration and a little trip to the West. My wife and I have just been halfway round the world and now we're on our way back to Poshlost for the official opening——

Anna —and jollification——

Anton —of my brand new tractor works.

Sergeant Such a great man! How ever can I make it up to you?

Anton Oh, very well, I suppose you were only doing your duty. The state has to be protected against unscrupulous spivs and smugglers. They're undermining us. Still, there is a small service you could render me.

Sergeant Just name it and it's done.

Anton And I won't see you unrewarded. I've not returned from the West without a few of life's little luxuries, eh, eh, get my drift? Anna, open the hatbox. (*Pause*) There, comrade. Take a look inside.

Sergeant Suffering Stalin!

Anton Yes, the forbidden fruits of the West. The stuff our Soviet dreams are made on. Razor blades . . . scented soap. Go on, take anything you like. All I ask in return is to travel in the luxury car.

Sergeant The luxury car?

Anton The Trans-Siberian Express carries a luxury car with gorgeous upholstery.

Anna A refrigerator stuffed with sturgeon and woodcock.

Anton It's reserved for the highest state luminaries. Even higher than me.

Sergeant I'm sorry. It can't be done, your honour.

Anton Can't be done? Anna, open the small suitcase. (*Pause*) Now, there!

Sergeant Good grief!

Anton American denims. Marks and Spencer woollens.

Anna Take your pick, comrade. A civic deputation is awaiting our triumphal return.

Anton We want to roll up superbly in the luxury car.

Sergeant But you're are asking the impossible.

Anna Anton, open the big suitcase.

Sergeant Please! Have mercy! You don't understand. The fact is the luxury car is reserved.

Anna But for whom?

Sergeant A commissar.

Anton Eh? Commissar of what?

Sergeant Chief Commissar of the People's Control Commission.

Anton But I don't understand.

Sergeant You must have heard about Comrade Gorbachev's fresh ideas.

Anton Fresh ideas? No, we've been in the West.

Sergeant Comrade Gorbachev ordered a massive crackdown on slackness and corruption and official incompetence. A purge of the party bigwigs out in the sticks who line their own pockets with the fat of the land. They reckon some of these fine fellows with high-sounding titles and ribbons in their button-holes do more fiddling than the Moscow State Orchestra. But not any more. Not when this commissar's finished with them.

Anton You don't say? Where is he going exactly?

Sergeant Who can tell? Popping in here, pouncing there, catching the villains with their hands in the till and their pants down. Lord forbid that I should ever live in a town where he chances to call, because all the culprits are going to be shot.

Anton Shot? Anna, shut that suitcase immediately. Come. It's time we were finding that daughter of ours.

Anton and Anna hurry off in one direction, the Sergeant exits in the other

Osip and Ivan stroll along

Osip Tell me something, comrade.

Ivan Yes?

Osip What exactly is your position in Siberia?

Ivan Delicate.

Osip Ah, you mean your lips are sealed.

Ivan You could say the Kremlin has sworn me to eternal silence.

Osip You must be terribly important.

Ivan Important? Yes, this is the only country where poetry is so important that they kill you for it.

Osip Poetry? I don't understand.

Ivan No, there's a great deal you don't understand. They say a tsadik never does.

Osip A tsadik? What's a tsadik?

Ivan A miracle worker. According to old Hebrew legend the Almighty places thirty-six tsadikim on the earth at any given time. They're God's understudies when he's taking a day off from his labours. To look at they're just thirty-six ordinary men going about their every day business. And they have no knowledge of their miraculous powers until the moment comes when only a miracle will do. Then wham, they make with the miracle.

Osip And you think I'm one of those? Are you crazy?

Ivan Crazy I might be but ten minutes ago I prayed for a miracle and when I looked around you were standing beside me.

Osip Are you joking?

Pause

Ivan Am I joking? How could there be miracles when the party tells us there's no God? You are a good party member, I take it?

Osip I put the party before everything, comrade. I'd die for it gladly.

Ivan Today you could get your wish.

Osip I beg your pardon?

Ivan *Gevalt!*

Osip What's the matter?

Ivan I've just been stabbed in the brain by the stiletto of an idea. If a man must go to hell he might as well go there in the luxury car.

Osip Ah, but comrade——

Ivan Tomorrow we could be fed to the wolves so today we live a little.

Osip But I thought the luxury car was reserved for party wigbigs.

Ivan Nonsense. It's never used. Since when did a party bigwig go willingly to Siberia? If a party bigwig goes to Siberia he's no longer a bigwig and he rides in the slave car.

Natasha and Sonya enter. They sit on the bench

Gevalt! First I meet a miracle worker and now two angels.

Osip What? Where?

Ivan Those two girls. What beauties. Come on.

Osip Where are we going?

Ivan To pick them up. This could be our last chance before we're swallowed in everlasting darkness. Come on. We'll use the classic ploy.

Osip What classic ploy?

Ivan The dropped handkerchief.

Osip How do you know they *will* drop their handkerchiefs?

Ivan Are you serious? In Russia the man drops the handkerchief. Now I'll tell you exactly what to do.

As Ivan instructs Osip in the art of picking up girls—with suitable gestures— the conversation of Natasha and Sonya sitting on the bench becomes audible

Sonya And did I tell you, Natasha? Last night I dreamed I'd been given a beautiful candy-striped tractor with a big blue satin bow on the bonnet.
Natasha And I dreamed that Count Vronsky had fallen in love with me.
Sonya Yes, it must have been the cheese.

Ivan and Osip approach

Natasha Sonya, look!
Sonya Men? Frankly I'd rather have a good steel garden fork.

Ivan and Osip drop their hankies and pass on

Natasha Good heavens, did you see that? Well come on!
Sonya I'm going nowhere.
Natasha All right, be an old maid all your life. (*She picks up Ivan's hankie and runs after him*)

Sonya picks up Osip's hankie and sits down again

Sir! Comrade! One moment please. Excuse me, sir, I believe you dropped this.
Ivan Good heavens, so I did. Thank you so much.
Natasha It's a pleasure. Tell me, are you off on a journey or are you meeting Anna?
Ivan Anna?
Natasha Oh, what a fool I am. I thought for a moment . . . no, it's so silly.
Ivan No, do go on.
Natasha I thought you were Count Vronsky. Oh, you must think I'm such a fool.
Ivan Not at all. But as you see, I'm nothing so grand. I'm a humble poet.
Natasha A poet! How fantastically wonderful.
Ivan Well, just a little wonderful. Shall we stroll on? May I take your arm?
Natasha I must be dreaming. Me—arm in arm with a poet—on the Yaroslavsky Station.

Osip comes back searching the ground for his handkerchief. He finally reaches the bench, where Sonya sits with loftily averted eyes

Osip Oh . . . erm . . . excuse me, comrade.
Sonya (*coldly*) Yes?
Osip I thought I'd better come back and see if you'd pick me up.
Sonya What!
Osip Picked it up.
Sonya Picked what up?
Osip My signal. No, my hand signal. No, my handkerchief.
Sonya The one you threw away?

Osip That's the one. I mean no. I mean the one I meant for you.

Sonya Oh, I've got that one. Thank you very much. Good linen hankies are as scarce as good garden tools where I come from.

Osip No, but you see I'd like it back. Tatiana made it for me on her sewing machine.

Sonya Your sweetheart?

Osip My sister. And Mother embroidered the little blue flowers in the corner. Delphiniums. Like your eyes.

Sonya You like flowers?

Osip Oh yes.

Sonya How about vegetables?

Osip Yes, those too, but not as much as delphiniums.

Sonya You grow them?

Osip Yes, Father says I'm a miracle worker with scarlet runners.

Sonya Sit down. Talk.

Osip Thank you.

Sonya Where do you grow?

Osip My father runs a state farm just south of Moscow. I help him out at harvest time.

Sonya Tell me, comrade, do you know how to get hold of a good steel garden fork?

Osip Oh yes.

Sonya You do?

Osip By the handle.

Sonya No no no. I mean could you steal one for me?

Osip What? Steal state property?

Sonya I've got a rather large private plot and most of my tools are held together with sticking plaster and pins.

Osip What? You have a private plot? But good heavens, that's capitalism. You're not just dishonest, you're—you're—you're counter-revolutionary.

Sonya Don't be ridiculous. I'd be happy if there was a world revolution tomorrow and Communism everywhere.

Osip Thank goodness for that.

Sonya Yes. Just as long as they left one little country with capitalism where we could go and have fun. (*Pause*) Well, what are you staring at?

Osip Your eyes. How could a girl with eyes like delphiniums be so blind?

There is the sound of the train drawing in

Natasha So this is goodbye, comrade.

Ivan But not for ever.

Natasha Oh, yes, once again my happiness is snatched away. It's my eternal fate.

Ivan But we're both going to Siberia. Tell me the name of your town— quickly.

Natasha Poshlost.

Ivan Posh?

Natasha Lost.

Anton ⎫
Anna ⎭ (*off, together*) Natasha! Natasha!

Natasha My parents. We must say goodbye. Farewell, comrade.

Natasha and Ivan kiss

Sonya Listen, there's my master calling. Here, take back your hankie.
Osip No, you keep it—please. It goes with your eyes.
Sonya What a funny boy. I'll think of you whenever I blow my nose.

Sonya and Osip hold hands—or rather the handkerchief

    Ivan tears himself away from Natasha and goes off. Anton and Anna enter

Anna (*embracing Natasha*) Natasha! Thank heavens!
Natasha (*in tears*) Oh, Mother! Momotchka!
Anton Natasha! My little Natushka. A big kiss for your daddy! Mmm!
    There! And now hurry—our carriage is right at the back of the train,
    damn it! (*He starts to go*)
Anna But where's that wretched girl Sonya?

    Anton, Anna and Natasha exit

Anton (*going*) Oh, hell's bells! Sonya! Sonya!
Sonya (*hurrying off*) Yes, I'm coming.

    Sonya exits. Ivan enters

Ivan (*hurrying to Osip*) Come on, come on, we've got to jump to it.
Osip Comrade, did you see her, did you see her?
Ivan I did, I did.
Osip Isn't she lovely?
Ivan She's a corker. And what was your girl like? Now hurry. The luxury
    car's right at the front of the train. Well come on!

    Ivan and Osip hurry off. The Militia Sergeant enters

Sergeant All right! Come on! Get those doors closed.

The train doors slam. The whistle blows. The train moves out

    And off they go. But wait. Where's the commissar? He never turned up.
    Oh, well, Siberia can sleep in peace.

The Lights fade to a Black-out

Scene 2

Poshlost station, Central Siberia. But no snow—this is summer

*Anton, Anna, Sonya and Natasha have just got off the train, which is still in the
station. A band plays off*

Sonya Home, home, home! Just smell the country air.

Natasha Just smell the vodka distillery.
Anna (*pointing off, up the platform*) Look, Anton, a band.
Sonya Yes, I wonder who it can be for?
Anna For me and your master, you dolt.
Sonya Oh, I thought somebody important had arrived.
Anton What a farce. What a spectacle. The town band blazing away at the front of the train while the party secretary and his family crawl out at the back like the wheeltapper and his apprentices. Well, I hope somebody's coming to carry all this luggage.

The train starts out and Natasha gazes off after it longingly

Natasha (*aside*) Goodbye, pitiless train, that carries my heart away for ever into the freezing steppe. I wonder if he'll wave to me.
Anna What did you say, Natasha?
Natasha Nothing, Mother. (*Aside*) No, he didn't even wave.
Anna Anton, there seems to be a fight going on up there.
Anton Yes, the vodka's been flowing. What's new about that? Come on, everybody pick up one suitcase and we'll walk.
Anna Are you out of your mind? The reception committee should rush to meet *us*.
Anton But Anna—this town—oh, it's all right, they've seen us. Here come Bobchinsky and Dobchinsky.

Bobchinsky and Dobchinsky rush on and embrace the new arrivals

Bobchinsky Greetings, Comrade Secretary.
Dobchinsky Welcome home, dear Anna Andreyevna.
Bobchinsky Natasha Antonovna.
Dobchinsky Sonya Alexandrovna.
Bobchinsky Anton Antonovich, what was it like in the West?
Anton Well——
Dobchinsky Natasha Antonovna, what was Moscow like?
Bobchinsky (*to Anton*) Don't you wish you'd stayed there?
Anton Well——
Dobchinsky (*to Natasha*) Did you bring home a husband?

Natasha stifles a sob and walks away offended

Bobchinsky (*to Dobchinsky*) Look what you've done now! Please be silent! Let me ask the questions. Anton Antonovich, tell us about all the ostentation of the rich, the oppression of the workers, the blatant militarism, the filth and corruption, the high living and low morality that you found in——
Dobchinsky That you found in Moscow.
Bobchinsky Yes, that you . . . no, no, no! That you found in the West.
Dobchinsky Found in the West.
Bobchinsky Be quiet, Dobchinsky!
Dobchinsky Yes, yes.
Bobchinsky Thank you. Dear Anton——
Dobchinsky I won't say another word.

Bobchinsky Dear Anton——
Dobchinsky Not one. Upon my soul.

Bobchinsky gives Dobchinsky a violent shove and he ends up next to a pigskin portmanteau

Anton Antonovich, please tell us about the West.

Anton The West, as you so rightly surmise, is totally corrupt. All they are interested in is piling up material possessions and luxury goods for mere ostentation and display. Dobchinsky! Put down that suitcase.

Dobchinsky I was only going to carry it for you, comrade.

Anton Well put it down!

Dobchinsky drops the case with a crash of breaking glass

It's full of Waterford crystal brandy balloons!

Dobchinsky (*lifting and shaking the suitcase*) So it is. No damage.

Bobchinsky But Comrade Secretary, is the West just as Charles Dickens paints it, or is——

Dobchinsky Or is *Oliver Twist* just a whitewash?

Bobchinsky Yes, the food queues, the workers' living space——

Dobchinsky Are they catching up with us?

Anton Comrades, I just can't tell you. As soon as you arrive they pull the wool over your eyes.

Dobchinsky Wool over your eyes. Just fancy that.

Anton Why, to give you just one example: we arrive in the West. Come to see one of our coal mines, they say. Comrades, we draw up in a vast parking space with gleaming new cars stretching to the horizon. Luxury models. But this is a car factory, I say. No, says my guide. All these cars belong to the coal miners. And that's how it went. One lie after another. And they could teach us a trick or two about dealing with dissident writers. They don't send them to lunatic asylums—no—they send them to the National Theatre and that foxes the beggars.

Dobchinsky That fixes the buggers.

Anton And then there was our hotel.

Anna Yes, but it was terribly smart, Anton.

Anton Just to impress us. The workers never get inside such places.

Anna We had a four-room suite with our own private bathroom tiled in primrose and cream. The toilet roll was kept in a pink woollen cosy.

Bobchinsky What's a cosy?

Dobchinsky What's a toilet roll?

Anton Never you mind. That's enough of your idiotic questions. I want to hear all about this fight.

Bobchinsky What fight?

Anton The drunken brawl that's just been going on up at the front of that blessed train.

Bobchinsky Oh, *that* fight. Well, you won't believe this, Anton Antonovich. The train drew up and the luxury car stopped exactly in line with us.

Dobchinsky And we were certain you'd be inside it because you said you had ways of sweetening the——

While all this is going on, the ever-practical Sonya loads the luggage on a trolley and wheels it off

Bobchinsky Please, Dobchinsky, I'm telling it.

Dobchinsky No, let me, Bobchinsky. You'll muddle it all up.

Bobchinsky But you'll leave out all the best bits, I know you will.

Anton In the name of Rasputin, come to the point!

Bobchinsky Allow me. Well, I awoke this morning and I said to myself, dear Anton Antonovich is coming home today, so I thought I'd go and get my best boots from the cobbler's.

Dobchinsky The one next door to the shop where they sell hot pies.

Bobchinsky Sell hot pies. Well, coming away from there who should I bump into but Dobchinsky. He'd been on some errand to Philip Antonovich Pochechuev. I can't remember what.

Dobchinsky To fetch a jug of vodka.

Bobchinsky A jug of vodka, yes, so we walked to the railway station.

Dobchinsky And he said——

Bobchinsky Please, Dobchinsky! Don't keep interrupting. I said, Let's go to the refreshment room, I've had nothing to eat today, my stomach's starting——

Dobchinsky —starting to revolve.

Bobchinsky —to revolve. No! To rumble. Please don't interrupt.

Anton Devil take your stomach! Get on with it!

Bobchinsky And so when the train drew in I was holding a pickled herring in my right hand——

Dobchinsky —and a glass of tea in his left hand.

Bobchinsky —and a glass of tea in my left hand. Or wait, I think it was the other way about.

Dobchinsky The herring was in the right hand.

Bobchinsky (*sniffing*) Oh yes, I can still smell it. It doesn't matter because I decided to go on board and give it to you because I thought——

Dobchinsky —he thought you'd be a bit peckish. He'd only taken one bite and a sip of tea.

Bobchinsky —one bite and a sip of tea.

Dobchinsky It was scalding hot.

Bobchinsky Please, Dobchinsky! Anyway, no sooner had we climbed into the luxury car than——

Anton Wait! You climbed into the luxury car? Jumping Saint Jude!

Bobchinsky Yes, no sooner had we climbed into the luxury car than I——

Dobchinsky Than he spilt the tea.

Bobchinsky Down the legs of the young man coming out.

Anton You spilt tea on him? Oh, no.

Bobchinsky But he said don't mind me at all. Yes, just fancy that.

Dobchinsky He had such good manners. Such a thoughtful expression.

Bobchinsky But just at that moment Colonel Bullbich appeared on the scene carrying a bouquet of carnations.

Dobchinsky No, no, a bunch of roses.

Bobchinsky Carnations.

Dobchinsky Roses.

Anton What? For the commissar? Smart thinking.

Dobchinsky No, no, for Natasha Antonovna.

Natasha For me? Oh, my God.

Bobchinsky Yes, he intended proposing marriage, he told me just last night, he thought he'd find you in the luxury car, but instead he found this strange young man——

Dobchinsky —with wet trousers.

Bobchinsky And he said to the young man, who the devil do you think you are to travel in such luxury?

Dobchinsky With wet trousers.

Bobchinsky Let me see your papers, he said. And the second young man said——

Anton What? There were two of them?

Bobchinsky Yes, there were two of them and they were travelling without tickets, without papers, without anything at all, except that one of them had a volume of Pushkin's poetry.

Dobchinsky Yes, Pushkin's poetry. Fancy that.

Anton My God. Travelling incognito. Mother of Stalin preserve us.

Natasha What was that? Did somebody say Pushkin?

Dobchinsky Yes, a poet. Highly thought of. But they shot him in the end, of course.

Anton Will you be quiet! This could be the death of all of us. Carry on, Bobchinsky.

Bobchinsky So Colonel Bullbich said to the ruffian with the book, who do you think you are to travel in such style, you lout? A commissar? And the young man pulled himself up and said yes, a commissar of the unquenchable human spirit. And the other one said he'd like to see all Poshlost damned.

Dobchinsky No, no, he said he'd like to see the Poshlost dam.

Bobchinsky What are you talking about? He said he'd see us damned.

Anton And so he will, and so he will.

Bobchinsky And that's when the fight started. A terrible scene. Black eyes, carnations trampled under foot.

Dobchinsky Rose petals flying hither and thither.

Anton Karl Marx have mercy! What did Bullbich do with them?

Dobchinsky He gave orders to put them in a bowl of fresh water, but the stalks were broken and there was hardly a petal unshed. But perhaps he could stick them on again with glue.

Anton No, no! Not the flaming flowers. What did he do with the commissar and his henchman?

Bobchinsky Ah, well after he'd overpowered them he dragged them straight off to the lunatic asylum.

Anton Oh yes?

Bobchinsky They were madmen, you see.

Anton Oh yes? That's splendid. You know what he's done? He's only dragged a commissar off to the loony bin, that's all.

Bobchinsky No, comrade, you misunderstand. He wasn't really a comm——

Anton But I tell you he is a commissar. I was tipped the wink in Moscow. He was aboard that train. Now quickly—Bobchinsky—off to that asylum. Cut through the cemetery. Stop them before they get their noses inside that mad house.

Bobchinsky Oh, you mean because of the nightgowns?

Anton Just run. Wait. What about the nightgowns?

Bobchinsky The wife of the chief psychiatrist had them all altered.

Anton The nightgowns?

Bobchinsky Yes, to sell as wedding dresses. (*He laughs maniacally*)

Anton Another racket! What a bunch of gangsters! Never mind the nightgowns. Just overtake them. Apologize. Grovel. Say it was all a dreadful mistake because I was absent abroad. Bring them to my house. Well run!

Bobchinsky Yes, at once. Oh, do you still want the pickled herring? It's in my back pocket keeping warm.

Anton Just run, you blockhead!

Bobchinsky runs off

There he goes, the principal of our university. (*Turning to Dobchinsky*) And this one's the chief justice of the district court. Now listen, my friend, we're in it up to our necks and it doesn't smell like roses.

Dobchinsky But surely, comrade——

Anton One glance at this town's enough to condemn us. The streets haven't been swept since Stalin's funeral. Round up all the population. Proclaim a compulsory day of voluntary communist labour. I want the whole place spotless by half-past two. Christ, look at the dome of the cathedral! A great hole in the side where these drunken Red Army gunners have been using it for target practice. And Lenin's statue, covered in verdigris. Looks like a mouldy lump of gorgonzola pointing the way forward to his maggots. I might as well put a bullet in my brain right now. With five hundred towns strung out along six thousand miles of railway line why do they have to step out here and terrorize us? Have we offended the Almighty?

Dobchinsky Who?

Anton No, there's no such person and that's official, God damn it.

Anna Anton, dear.

Anton Yes?

Anna You're forgetting the holy icons.

Anton By the bones of Saint Basil, they'll want to inspect the holy icons. No, they'll want to grab them as a perk. They're no better than highway robbers. And what time is it? Oh, lord, Father Sergius will be celebrating mass. I gave him permission to carry on preaching in return for letting me smuggle the icons to the West. Dobchinsky, get that priest out of the way. Brick him up in the crypt and make sure the cathedral looks respectable. Hide all the prayer books. Now what else is there?

Anna Stalin's collected works.

Anton Stalin's collected works?

Anna They're still on the shelves in the public library.

Anton Thunder and damnation, so they are. And so are Khruschev's. We never got round to burning them. Yes, we'll make a bonfire of 'em in the tractor factory.

Dobchinsky The tractor factory? But comrade——

Anton Yes, the tractor factory! Well, run! Stop! Better burn Brezhnev's and Andropov's while we're about it. I don't know if they're banned yet but it's best to play safe. And fill the place with the glorious works of Comrade Gorbachev—if he's written any. Is that all? It'll have to be. Well, come on, Anna, what are you waiting for? I want the best bedrooms prepared. Great ships need deep water, you know.

Anton, Anna and Dobchinsky hurry off

The Lights fade to a Black-out

SCENE 3

A sitting-room in Anton's house

There are over-stuffed chairs, silk tasselled lampshades and a portrait of Lenin

Anna sweeps in, pleased about something, followed by Natasha

Anna (*entering*) So we're to have men in the house. Imagine that. Suave, distinguished, powerful men, from Moscow. Under my roof. Sleeping in my guest bedroom.

Natasha (*in her own dream*) One of them reads Pushkin, Mamushka. Did you ever hear of such a thing?

Anna In Poshlost? Never. Such good manners, Dobchinsky said. Such a thoughtful expression. But what will he make of me? Such men have an instinctive eye for quality. And I'm told I hardly look old enough to have a child of sixteen.

Natasha Sixteen? Mother, I'm twenty-two.

Anna Hush! Don't breathe a word of it. Pretend to be a minor, my darling, and they won't molest you. Men like this can be perfect brutes and take the most astonishing liberties. Leave all that to me. I've had experience in these things. Why, even in England the men couldn't resist winking their eye at me. And in France I received several absolutely outrageous proposals. And in Italy—oh, dear, I couldn't possibly tell you what those terrible Italians did.

Sonya enters

Sonya Goose, madam?

Anna Good heavens, how did you know?

Sonya We always have goose on Saturdays.

Anna Oh, the dinner. Yes, I see. No, we'll start with oysters, and then prime
beef steaks with plenty of vegetables. Bring out the silver.

Sonya starts to go

Oh, and Sonya, would you unpack the lingerie I bought at Dorothy
Perkins and lay it on my bed? Careful, it might blow away. Imagine, it's
so flimsy it looks exactly like the paper they wrap oranges in.

Sonya Sounds just right for the Siberian winter.

As Sonya goes she passes Anton, who is hurrying in

Anton Not a sign of them. That bonehead Bullbich could have beaten their
brains out by now. (*He pours and gulps a drink*) No, no, I'm letting my
imagination run away with me. They'll be here shortly. All will be well.
Just stay calm, that's all, and we'll get away with this, I know we will. No
need to be jumpy. Above all, don't flap. Oh, my God, they're here!

Sonya enters

Sonya Colonel Bullbich. (*She remains by the door*)

Bullbich enters carrying a damaged bunch of roses

Bullbich (*entering with arms outstretched*) Welcome home, dear friends.
How Poshlost has missed you all.

Anton My God, that black eye.

Bullbich Yes, just a little incident at the railway station.

Anton Little incident! He doesn't know! He doesn't know! Listen,
Bullbich——

Bullbich Do excuse me. I have a pleasant duty to perform.

Anton But Bullbich——

Bullbich (*glaring*) Please! (*He heads for Natasha*) Dear Natasha Antonovna,
may I present you with this little bunch of roses? I had them specially
imported from Odessa. They cost thirty-four and a half roubles.

Anna (*grabbing the flowers*) But Colonel, how devastatingly charming.
How can I accept such a present?

Bullbich But Anna Andreyevna——

Anna No, you'll have my husband jealous. Give them to Natasha instead.
Well, at least give her one of them. Here, darling, a rose from Stepan
Bullbich.

Natasha Thank you, Mother.

Anna Look out, there's a little worm in that one. But mine are quite
adorable, Colonel, it's so kind of you.

Bullbich (*taking Natasha aside*) Natasha Antonovna, you promised me an
answer.

Natasha Please, Colonel, I've only just arrived home. Let me get my breath
back.

Bullbich But don't forget who signed your travel permit. Remember that
without my permission you must stay in this town for ever. You won't
regret marrying me. I'm getting a new house. I'm going to Lower
Shalyapin Street.

Sonya (*aside*) Yes and if you stay there long enough you will.

Anton Enough of this! Bullbich, you won't be going to Lower Shalyapin Street. You'll be going to the Gulag. And about time, too. Yes!

Bullbich What are you talking about?

Anton Didn't you meet Bobchinsky—at the lunatic asylum?

Bullbich Bobchinsky? No.

Anton He didn't stop you? What did you do with them?

Bullbich I tucked them up warm.

Anton Warm?

Bullbich In straitwaistcoats. That asylum's been like an icebox ever since I started having the coal re-directed to my house. That's another thing, Natasha, you'll always be warm with me.

Anton Coal supplies? What? Another racket! All this is going to be exposed. That's why they're here. We fell right into their trap. We're dead Muscovy ducks, all of us. Our goose is cooked.

Bullbich Anton Antonovich, something seems to be troubling you.

Anton Oh no. No no no. I'm just going mad, that's all. Would you like to know why? You've just thrown a commissar into the madhouse.

Bullbich A commissar? Oh, no, my friend.

Anton Oh, yes, my friend. I was warned about him in Moscow. He's a genuine commissar. He was on our train. He's now in the lunatic asylum. He will soon be in this room. We will soon be swinging from those rafters. And a good thing, too. They'll have us for breakfast and our women for supper. Our women! My daughter! Natasha, go and hide under the bed. Take Sonya with you.

Natasha Oh, but Father——

Anton Go!

Natasha and Sonya leave

The sight of female flesh sets men such as this in a frenzy.

Bullbich In that case shouldn't Anna leave too?

Anna No, I'll stay, I'll stay. Let them do their worst.

Anton You're a good wife, Anna. I'm sure I don't deserve you.

Bullbich I'm still not convinced.

Anton Not convinced?

Bullbich That we're dealing with a commissar. He's much too young.

Anton Well of course he's a commissar. You heard it from his own lips.

Bullbich (*taking a scrap of paper from his pocket*) Yes, but what about this list of instructions? It's very fishy to me.

Anton What list of instructions?

Bullbich That I found in the pocket of the commissar's assistant.

Anton Why? What does it say?

Bullbich (*reading*) "Eat up all your vegetables; brush your teeth after meals; scrub your nails; clean socks every day; clean underwear Mondays and Thursdays; wash under your armpits; wash your neck; wash between your——

Anton Yes yes yes. It's obviously some kind of code. Comrade Gorbachev is damnably subtle.

Bullbich It isn't signed Gorbachev. It's signed Mummy.

Anton I tell you it's a code, a secret code!

There is a banging on the door

Oh, God help us! They're here. Calm, everybody. Don't flap. We have nothing to hide. Yes! (*Calling out*) Come in!

Bobchinsky and Dobchinsky enter, followed by Ivan and Osip. Bobchinsky's clothes are covered with graveyard clay

Anton Ah, Bobchinsky and Dobchinsky. And two friends, I see. Won't you all come in? Won't you perform the introductions, Bobchinsky?

Bobchinsky Anton Antonovich, we were too late to prevent these unfortunate gentlemen being——

Dobchinsky —being strapped into straitwaistcoats and dosed with castor oil.

Bobchinsky Oh, do let me, Dobchinsky! You weren't even there! You see, I was hurrying through the cemetery as fast as my legs would carry me and unfortunately I couldn't take my eyes off the fine new cross in red marble they were erecting for old Koozma Nikolayevich——

Dobchinsky God rest his soul.

Bobchinsky And I stumbled over one of those cast-iron flower urns, yes——

Dobchinsky —and fell right into an open grave.

Bobchinsky And fell right into——

Anton Please! I said won't you introduce these gentlemen.

Ivan Allow me to introduce myself. My name is Ivan Alexandrovich Khlestakov, poet. And this is Osip Konstantinovich Shipoochkin.

Anton (*aside*) A poet! Well there's a fine incognito for you. (*Aloud*) We esteem your visit a great honour, comrades. I am Party Secretary Anton Antonovich Skvoznik Dmukhanovsky and this is my good wife Anna Andreyevna.

Anna Our simple home is yours, gentlemen.

Anton We extend every hospitality this little town can afford.

Ivan Spare the sarcasm, if you please.

Anton Sarcasm? Oh, you mean the straitwaistcoats, but that was nothing more than an excess of zeal, sir, on the part of a notoriously keen and efficient militia. Unfortunately they took you to the wrong place. It's for enemies of the people, you know.

Ivan Then why is it full of our biggest hearts and brightest minds and best people? And how can Russia climb its Everest if it buries all its mountaineers?

Anton I—I beg your pardon?

Ivan Oh, don't think you can silence me. I've nothing to lose now so I'll unload my tongue. But first you can let my friend go. He's here on different business.

Anton Different business?

Ivan Tell them Osip.

Osip Oh—well—yes—I've come to dam the building.

Anton Good lord, which building? (*Aside*) Did you hear that, Bullbich?

He's a building inspector. But at least he doesn't mince words and pretend to be what he isn't like the other one. (*Aloud*) Er, which building do you have in mind, comrade? We have several which are ripe for, er, condemnation.

Osip No, the *dam* building.

Anton (*aside*) He's not just frank, he's downright rude.

Ivan Osip Konstantinovich means the hydroelectric dam.

Anton The dam? But you can't damn that. I mean, there's nothing there to be damned. Wouldn't you rather damn, er, well let me see, the cathedral?

Osip Why, is it flooded?

Anton Not as far as I'm aware. (*Aside*) Anna, I'm drowning.

Anna (*aside*) Stop trying to bandy words with him. Let him go and see the dam. Sonya can take him. It's all her fault. I'll fetch her. (*Aloud*) Excuse me, gentlemen.

Anna goes out, closing the door behind her

Anton A bite to eat before you go, Osip Konstantinovich? A dish of ham soup perhaps?

Osip No thank you.

Bobchinsky You wouldn't care for a pickled herring?

Dobchinsky Slightly damaged?

Osip No thank you.

Anton Name just anything that comes to mind. We keep a first-class pantry.

The door opens and Sonya enters with Anna

Sonya You wished to see me? Good heavens! It's you!

Osip Delphiniums!

Anton Delphiniums? How would you like them served? On a sandwich?

Bobchinsky | (*together*   Poached? Fried? Boiled? Toasted?
Dobchinsky | *variously*)

Anna Sonya, this comrade's come from Moscow to inspect the dam.

Sonya The dam? (*She laughs*) Which dam?

Anton That's enough of that. Just take him there. Show him. Explain.

Sonya (*laughing*) Explain about the dam?

Anna Sonya, kindly control yourself.

Sonya Sorry. Follow me, comrade. (*She opens the door*) After you, comrade.

Osip Thank you.

Osip exits, followed by Sonya, who whoops with laughter as she goes

Ivan Very well. I'd like everything settled at once. (*Pause*) Well, what's it to be? The bullet or the hemp necklace? Or is there some local refinement you'd prefer such as being sliced thinly from the toes up? (*Pause*) Have you nothing to say, Mr Party Secretary?

Anton (*gulping*) Only that—well—it's very sporting of you to give me the choice.

Ivan I said spare the sarcasm. I want the sentence carried out at once.

Anton What? Before I have time to make my peace with the Almighty?

Ivan (*aside*) What have we here? A Siberian satirist?

Anna Sir, have mercy! Oh, why do you have to inflict yourself on this little out of the way town when you have all the world to choose from?

Ivan All the world? Dear lady, aren't you forgetting a little matter of five thousand roubles?

Pause

Anna Would you mind repeating that?

Ivan A little matter of five thousand roubles. (*Pause*) So why the big saucer eyes?

Anton But we've never heard it spoken of so openly. We're simple, old fashioned folk. We're used to certain formalities in these affairs. For example——Ah! Ivan Alexandrovich, stand still a moment!

Ivan What is it? I never moved.

Anton No, but there's a patch of white dust on your coat. Do you see it, Bobchinsky?

Bobchinsky Without doubt it's a patch of white dust. Tt-tt-tt!

Dobchinsky In the region of the hip pocket.

Anna Anton, dear, you'd better brush it off.

Ivan Keep away from me! What stupid game are you playing?

Anton Just stand still, my friend, while I dust you down.

Ivan Keep your filthy paws off me!

Anton Patience, patience.

Ivan There's something in your hand.

Anton You're imagining things.

Ivan But look—you've dropped a pile of roubles.

Anton Me? You're mistaken, sir. That must be yours. But perhaps you'd like a few moments alone to collect it all. I mean to collect yourself. Come, Anna.

Anton, Anna, Bobchinsky, Dobchinsky and Colonel Bullbich troop out

Ivan Roubles. Hundreds of them. Thousands. Five, ten, fifteen. One thousand, two, three, four . . . five thousand roubles!

The door bursts open; Natasha enters and slams it shut

Natasha So there you are! And you've taken your thirty pieces of silver.

Ivan *Gevalt!* Natasha, what are you doing here?

Natasha I live here. Poet? No, crook! Deceiver!

Ivan But Natasha——

Natasha Don't speak my name. You've already polluted the very railway station that my heart held holy, so leave my name untarnished or I'll change it for another.

Ivan But listen——

Natasha To more lies? No. Oh, I might have had a copeck's worth of respect for you if you'd stayed here and done your duty like a gentleman—even if we'd all suffered for it—but to be a liar, a boaster, a bribe taker!

Ivan Wait. My duty? What duty?

Natasha It's no good pretending. You're a commissar for all the world to see—and you're utterly base.

Ivan Base I might be. We all have our off-moments. But a commissar? Me?

Natasha A poet! And I believed every word. How could I be so naïve? And you told the same lie to my parents and they weren't taken in for a second. I know because I was listening at the keyhole.

Ivan But I can explain.

Natasha (*hopefully*) You can?

Ivan (*aside*) Hold everything. Where does that leave me?

Natasha I'm waiting!

Ivan God, if only I could tell you the truth.

Natasha If only a deaf man could tune a piano!

Ivan But Natasha——

Natasha I've only one more thing to say. You may hang me from these rafters, comrade. You may take me out and shoot me. You may slice me thinly from the toes up. But if you must masquerade in false feathers as part of your sneaky trade, never again dishonour the glorious name of poet or I'll rise from the grave and you'll never have another moment's rest! Good-night!

Natasha rushes out, sobbing

Pause

Ivan (*to the sky*) Hello—God? Can you hear me up there? Listen, I knew you had a sense of the ridiculous but this time you really over-spiced the goulash. A Jewish, dissident, satirical, poetical *commissar*? Oy oy oy! (*Pause*) Wait. What am I dreaming of? The Red Sea is parted. I've been given a clear run to the West. Freedom! (*He starts to go off then pauses and comes back*) No, first there's something else I must do. To give thanks to the Lord. And my text is taken from Isaiah, chapter sixty-one, verse one: "The Lord hath sent me to proclaim liberty to the captive and an opening of the door to them that are bound." Yes, the prisoners. I can free the prisoners from the madhouse. I can do anything I like. I'm a commissar. What a situation. I'll stay just long enough to turn this little town on its head, to topple the mighty, to raise up the meek, to spread a little crazy mischief. And who knows, maybe to make a little love. Yes, I'll do it, I'll do it! (*He barks at the door*) Anton Antonovich! Colonel Bullbich! In here! At the double!

The Lights fade to a Black-out

SCENE 4

A hilltop just outside Poshlost

Sonya and Osip enter

Sonya Come on, comrade, hurry, before the sun goes down.

Osip Where are we?

Sonya The highest hill in Poshlost. Now—there—look.

Osip (*whistling in admiration*) Good heavens.

Sonya Isn't it wonderful?

Osip What a valley. What crops.

Sonya Every inch bursting with vegetables and cereals.

Osip This even beats my father's place.

Sonya We planted everything with our bare hands. Just imagine what we could do with good strong tools. Even so it's the only place in Poshlost that works properly. It's a magnet for the sun and it's watered by a tributary of the Posh. It's sheltered from wind and storm by that great belt of birches, you see? When I was a girl it was a wilderness. My father ran two cows and half a dozen sheep on it. We started reclaiming it from the swamp just ten years ago, and now the soil's so sweet you could bake it with nuts and cherries and eat it with cream. Only I wouldn't let you, comrade, because we don't waste a crumb. The growing season's too short. That's why all the little workers are still in the fields at this hour.

Osip Yes, why have you got the fidgets?

Sonya The fidgets?

Osip The digits. Down there tilling and toiling.

Sonya Digits? Fidgets? Do you mean midgets?

Osip Yes, the tiny tillers totting away down there.

Sonya They're not midgets. Look closer, comrade. They're children.

Osip What? You mean such tiny toils have to tot away till this time on the collective?

Sonya Have you been on plum vodka?

Osip No, why?

Sonya I can't follow you.

Osip Why do you employ such tiny tots on the collective?

Sonya (*offended*) What do you mean, collective? This is my private plot.

Osip Private plot? (*He laughs*) Now come. You're pegging my rug.

Sonya Pegging your rug?

Osip Lulling my peg.

Sonya Oh, pulling your leg. I'm getting the hang of this. No, no, it's true. This is my private plot.

Osip But that's terrible. You're nothing but a spanker—a gesticulator.

Sonya What? (*She thinks and grows angry*) Gangster! Speculator? Now listen, don't you call *me* names. Even if you could get your tongue round them.

Osip But you're exploiting labour—and child labour at that. What a fascist! You'll be shot for this.

Sonya And I suppose you'll carry out the sentence personally.

Osip Gladly! (*Pause*) All right, now take me to the dam.

Sonya What? (*Laughing*) Do you mean you still don't understand?

Osip All right, what's so amusing?

Sonya Don't you see? This *is* the dam.

Osip What do you mean?

Sonya Right in front of you. This valley.

Osip Oh, no.

Sonya Can you imagine? They were going to flood my private plot. So we diverted the river. Who asked them for a dam? Nobody. Some crawling careerist in the Kremlin stuck a pin in a blank piece of Siberia and ordained a dam so he could climb up the ladder while we all died of scurvy by bright electric light.

Osip You diverted the river? Well you'll just have to bring it back, that's all.

Sonya Over my dead body.

Osip If necessary. You know what Lenin said?

Sonya I never met him.

Osip He said Communism is Soviet power plus electrification.

Sonya Tell him Communism is also two hundred and fifty million people queueing up for vegetables.

Osip Listen, comrade, wherever a waterfall rushes down or a mighty river rolls its waters, there shall we build electric power stations, true light-houses of socialized labour. Russia has freed herself forever from the yoke of the exploiter. Our task now is to light her way by an unquenchable glow of electric fires.

Pause

Sonya Good heavens, you just galloped across an entire paragraph without falling off once. But what's so amazing about that? You sucked in slogans from your mother's dugs.

Osip I beg your pardon!

Sonya You lapped up the party line with every spoonful of cabbage soup. It's only thinking for yourself that twists your tongue, isn't it?

Osip You take that back!

Sonya Oh, go pick the nits out of Lenin's beard.

Osip You take it back or I'll—or I'll—ooh!

Sonya You're already going to shoot me so what else can you do, Comrade Commissar?

Sonya marches off

Osip (*gazing after her in bewilderment*) Commissar?

The Lights fade to a Black-out

SCENE 5

Anton's sitting room

Ivan is pacing up and down

The door opens and Osip rushes in

Osip (*out of breath*) Comrade, there's something funny going on in this town.

Ivan It gets funnier from now on.

Osip You know that girl? The one with the delphiniums? She's got midgets.

Ivan Midgets?

Osip She took me to the dam, and you'll never believe this, but it wasn't there. And she's not just a cake, she's cruised.

Ivan Not just a crook?

Osip No, she's crazed. She's taken it into her head that I'm a commissar.

Ivan Well so you are, my friend. So relax. Enjoy.

Osip Pardon? Enjoy what?

Ivan Your promotion. *Mazel tov!* You've been made a commissar.

Osip You're as crazy as the rest of them, aren't you?

Ivan Why, what have the rest of them done?

Osip They all bowed to me when I just walked in.

Ivan What do you expect if you threaten to shoot the maid?

Osip Me?

Ivan She just rushed in here and said so.

Osip Shoot the . . . but surely she didn't take that seriously?

Ivan Who takes a commissar lightly?

Osip Don't keep saying that!

Ivan Are you telling me the job's too big for you? They'll be very disappointed in the Kremlin.

Osip You mean it's true? But why me?

Ivan We've been waiting for a giant and now he's arrived. First Ivan the Terrible. Then Peter the Great. And next?

Osip Yes?

Ivan Osip the Terribly Great.

Osip That's nonsense—isn't it?

Ivan No false modesty. You've been noticed and that's why you were sent here.

Osip But what for, comrade?

Ivan This town's been chosen—and so have you—for an experiment which could change the face of Russia. The Soviet family's in danger of breaking up. The children are weary of forever looking over their shoulders in fear of a tyrannical papa who's lost all touch with reality. Our little sisters— Poland, Hungary, Czechoslovakia, the Ukraine—are demanding to wear lipstick and eye shadow and go dancing on their own. The very house is rocking on its heels. It cries out for new builders, new architects. And that's where you come in. Osip, my friend, you've been chosen to build the model of a better house, one with big windows to let in the sun and ever-open doors so the children can fly away and come back whenever they like.

Osip But comrade——

Ivan But why start here, you ask. This stinking fleapit where you'd have to gallop for three years before reaching another town? Secrecy, Osip. Only a handful of the very top leaders are in the know. If the Kremlin old guard caught wind of this, they'd bring up all the big guns for a counter-attack, because they're terrified of change. It would threaten their warm seats.

Osip Do you mean we'll be parting from Communism?

Ivan Parting from it? We'll be restoring it to its old aims and ideals. Come over here. Look out of the window. (*Pause*) What do you see?

Osip Lenin's statue.

Ivan You've got to walk up to that statue and scrape off the layers of green mould and black corruption that have been building up for sixty years. You've got to get back to the shining metal of the revolution. Well, are you the man for the job, Osip?

Pause

Osip I'll need a uniform.
Ivan (*amazed and disturbed*) A uniform?
Osip Silver buttons.
Ivan Silver buttons? Nothing else? Not maybe a nice set of medals for the chest?
Osip Medals? Could I really?
Ivan Why not? To a commissar all is possible.

Pause

Osip Comrade?
Ivan Yes?
Osip How long would it take me to grow a Stalin moustache?
Ivan Oy oy oy! Now just pay attention. Your appointment will be pro-claimed tomorrow at the opening of the new tractor factory. All the town will be there. Then Anton Antonovich will make a full confession of all his crimes and errors and hand Poshlost over to you.
Osip To me? But of course I'll have you to lean on, to help, to advise.
Ivan Alas, no.
Osip No?
Ivan I'd give all I possess to stay and see what becomes of you but very sadly I have to travel on tomorrow.
Osip Oh, dear. Where are you going?
Ivan In a westerly direction.
Osip But all on my own ... I'll never cope. Frankly, I'm not cut out for giving orders, no matter how many moustaches you pin on my chest—I mean medals on my nose ... there, you see what I mean.
Ivan Not to worry. That's all been arranged. I've found a team of thirty-four honest men to give you all the help you need.
Osip Thirty-four? Yes, even I should manage with thirty-four helpers. Good men, are they?
Ivan The best, the bravest, the brightest that Poshlost has to offer.
Osip Really? Where did you find such men?
Ivan They were all assembled in one place.
Osip Oh? Which place was that?
Ivan Just where you'd expect to find the pick of Poshlost. In the madhouse.

The Lights fade to a Black-out

SCENE 6

Poshlost town square

Anton is on a bunting-swagged podium, addressing the townspeople, who are still applauding Ivan, who has just made the proclamation. The platform party also includes Anna, Bullbich, Bobchinsky, and Dobchinsky

Anton shakes the hand of Ivan

Anton Thank you, comrades, thank you, thank you, thank you! So there you have it, comrades. Ivan Ivanovich has spoken. You all came here this morning for the opening of our new tractor works but instead you are witnessing the opening of a sublime new page in the history of our town.

There is scattered applause from the crowd

No more bribery. No dishonesty. No fiddling of statistics. No banned books. No man punished for voicing unpopular opinion. Liberty to worship.

Girl Hallelujah!

Anton Amen, comrade! Yes, it's no longer a crime to shout amen and hallelujah. God has come out of the Gulag and is living in Poshlost.

Crowd Amen! Hallelujah! God be praised!

Anton When I first heard why the commissars were here, I smacked my forehead and said, "But this is what I've always wanted. What I've always thought but was too frightened to say". Before today, comrades, whenever I was tempted to make a subversive remark I talked to the cat. We all talked to the cat! Oh, you Russian pussies, if only you could speak! And so I lied and smiled and kept my thoughts to myself—and the cat. And I set myself up as a regular Caligula. Because of me, people were afraid of doing anything at all in our town. Afraid of talking above a whisper, of writing letters, of making new friends. And all the time, comrades, as I was laying down the law and punishing honest men, I was giving and taking bribes and cooking the books and faking government returns to suggest we were keeping abreast of the targets laid down in the five year plan.

There is a great indrawn breath from the crowd

Yes! Only a month ago Boris Petrovich of the ballbearing works came to me and said: "Anton Antonovich, our production chart shows a steeply falling production curve. What can we do?" And I replied, "Boris Petrovich, take the chart from the wall and put it back upside down. Then the curve will rise."

The crowd laughs at this one

It's not amusing, comrades! Under my leadership the economy of our town stagnated. The virtues of hard work and discipline were neglected. And how did I set an example? By running the best pantry in Poshlost and keeping the finest plum vodka for myself. By setting myself up as a King of caviare. By living la Bolshie vita! "But Anton Antonovich," you might say. "What about your heroic achievements? Behold the chimneys of our brand new tractor works merrily smoking. How on earth did you manage that when it's well known that all the components had to come two thousand miles by rail and were cannibalized at every stop along the line—by towns trying to fulfil *their* five year plan? How did you succeed when every time you required a dozen two inch screws you had to indent for a monster mobile crane—and take the leavings? That makes your triumph doubly glorious," you might say. "And that is why you so richly deserve the ribbon of the Order of Lenin which shines so proudly in your buttonhole this morning." Comrades! I rip the ribbon from my breast! Because I'm going to ask Bobchinsky and Dobchinsky to roll open the doors of our beautiful tractor works—and reveal the truth.

Bobchinsky Us? What a great honour? May I just say in gratitude——

Dobchinsky —how exceedingly proud and happy it makes us to declare——

Bobchinsky —yes, to declare this wonderful monument of Soviet achievement——

Dobchinsky —well and truly open.

Bobchinsky Yes!

Anton Well go on then! Open the flaming thing!

Bobchinsky ⎱
Dobchinsky ⎰ (*together*) Oh, yes, yes, yes, yes.

Bobchinsky and Dobchinsky hurry off

Anton looks up to heaven. The rumbling of two great steel doors sliding apart is heard

After a moment Bobchinsky and Dobchinsky return

Bobchinsky Comrade, there seems to be some mistake.

Dobchinsky We must have opened the wrong door.

Bobchinsky There's nothing inside there.

Dobchinsky No machinery.

Bobchinsky Nothing at all.

Dobchinsky Just an empty shell.

Bobchinsky Just four bare walls and a great bonfire burning in the middle of a bare floor.

Anton Yes, comrades, it's nothing but an empty shell with four chimneys on top belching forth a bonfire of banned books! That's our tractor factory for you. A fake! A sham! Just like me!

A band strikes up. Anton breaks down and sobs

Bobchinsky, Dobchinsky and Bullbich lead Anton off with murmurs of "What?" "Oh, lor'" "Good heavens!"

Anna stays behind

Anna (*straight at the audience*) Oh, the humiliation! I knew I was married to a stringless balalaika. But this!

Anna sweeps off

Osip enters, gorgeously uniformed and bemedalled

Ivan goes to greet him

Ivan Well goodbye, Osip. I must be leaving. My train's due in five minutes.
Osip Are you sure you can't stay?
Ivan It would be bad for my health. The climate, you know.
Osip What do you think of my uniform? You don't think all this gold braid's—well—a bit much?
Ivan On you it's becoming.

Sonya enters

Osip Really? Oh, look, there's Sonya Alexandrovna! I must have a word with her. (*Approaching Sonya*) Sonya, wait!
Sonya What do you want?
Osip A serious talk.
Sonya How can you talk seriously when you're wearing Peter Karpov's uniform?
Osip Who's Peter Karpov?
Sonya The cinema commissionaire. Just say your say.
Osip Comrade, I'm willing to make a compromise with you. I can't let you keep your private plot because the valley must be flooded, but I can let you have a private cucumber frame and a window-box.
Sonya I'd rather have a shroud and a pinewood box. Why not simply shoot me?
Osip Now don't be like that.
Sonya I fully admit to plotting privately. I plead guilty to potatoes. So shoot me.
Osip Come back here!
Sonya I confess to cabbages!

Sonya exits

Osip Sonya—but listen—Sonya! (*To Ivan*) Goodbye, comrade.
Ivan Goodbye, Osip.

Osip exits

As Ivan is about to exit, Natasha enters and hurries to him. She carries a book of poetry

Natasha Comrade! Ivan Alexandrovich. May I have a word?
Ivan Natasha! I'd be delighted.
Natasha You left this behind. A volume of Pushkin's verse. Part of your props, I presume, like a false moustache. Oh, how I despise a man who uses poetry for evil ends.
Ivan Tell me, what do you use it for?
Natasha To teach me how to live. Oh, you wouldn't understand.
Ivan So explain.
Natasha A poet can express those—oh, I don't know—he can put into words those elusive feelings ... those ...
Ivan Those half-grasped thoughts too subtle to say.
Natasha Why yes. How did you know?
Ivan You said it, more or less. But what kind of thoughts?

Natasha Thoughts such as—such as—oh—how one can despise some-body's views, his character, his whole way of life, and yet find oneself mysteriously drawn to him.

Ivan I've dipped into this Pushkin—just to flesh out my incognito, you understand. He has a trick of putting airy fairy matters quite bluntly and making you blink. For example, to convey the feeling you just mentioned he says, "This bread is stale and mouldy, even the dogs won't touch it, but the sight of it makes me ravenous and I want to devour it in one gulp."

Natasha Yes, exactly! But wait. Pushkin never said that. I know him by heart.

Ivan Maybe it was Blok—or Lermontov. And maybe it wasn't bread. Maybe it was herring.

Natasha (*indignantly*) Herring?

Ivan "Then why is it my ardent wish to gobble up this stinking fish?"

A train is heard in the distance

Natasha That is the most appalling doggerel.

Ivan Oh, my apologies.

Natasha There's your train. What a pity it can't carry you right out of Russia and bring back one of our banished poets in your place.

Ivan Who can tell, there might be a poet on board, going into happy exile.

Natasha Don't speak of what you don't know! A true poet would never willingly leave his native land—even a land that spits on the human spirit and tramples poetry in the dust.

Ivan Staying is so simple if the poet happens to be a carrion crow and caw-caw-caws the party line.

Natasha What do you mean?

Ivan Only sweet voiced birds are imprisoned. Crows are not kept in cages.

Natasha (*deeply puzzled*) What are you trying to say?

Ivan (*going*) Goodbye, Natasha.

Natasha Comrade, your book!

Ivan (*distantly*) Keep it. What's poetry to me? Goodbye.

Ivan exits

Natasha (*to herself, in tears*) Goodbye. Goodbye, stinking fish.

Bullbich enters

Bullbich Natasha! Natasha Antonovna, there you are.

Natasha Oh, Colonel.

Bullbich Natasha Antonovna, you promised me an answer.

Natasha Yes, of course, of course I did.

Bullbich Well, my dear?

Natasha The answer is yes. (*Sobbing*) Yes, yes, yes!

Bullbich Darling! Oh, these tears of happiness! Shush-shush-shush. Here, I've a little present for you, see? It's a gold locket. Well, almost gold. It cost seventy-six roubles all but a few copecks. There—it has my portrait in one of the little hearts. Here, let me put it round your pretty neck.

The Lights fade to a Black-out

ACT II

Anton's dining-room

Anna and Natasha are with Anton

Anton I tell you, Anna Andreyevna, you must do something about that girl
Sonya. A full week and she's refused to serve vegetables while the
commissar sits at this table. A man with the power of life or death.

Anna That's all right, Anton, vegetables will be served tonight. I stood over
her in the kitchen while she cooked them. Natasha, dear, start laying the
table, will you?

Natasha (*tearfully*) Yes, Mother.

Anna And stop that eternal weeping. You're going to be a bride.

Anton What a week! What an infernally amazing week! Seven days with a
commissar under our roof and still we survive to tell the tale. If you'd told
me last Saturday that in seven days' time this town would be run by a gang
of lunatics led by a young shaver who can't speak two straight sentences,
Anna Andreyevna, I'd have said you were a candidate for a straitwaist-
coat. If you'd told me that for the first time in memory this town would be
throbbing with industry and the streets swept and Lenin's statue shining
as bright as my grandad's gold watch, I'd have advised you to lie down at
once. Who'd have thought that bribery and drunkenness would be
unknown and the tractor factory about to give birth; that I'd be the night
foreman and Colonel Bullbich a traffic sergeant, well, Anna Andreyevna
I——

The door bursts open and Bullbich rushes in angrily

Bullbich Anton Antonovich, I must talk to you at once!

Anton You're covered in mud, Bullbich.

Bullbich Anton Antonovich, enough is enough! I refuse to stand in the
middle of the market place to be splashed by every passing motorist.

Anton What else can you expect? For years you penalized them for
imaginary offences and put the fines in your own pocket.

Bullbich But that's not all! There's something fishy about this experiment.
Do you realize there's talk of free elections? That can't be right for a start.
Well, I'm going to contact Moscow right away and question this
commissar's credentials.

Anton You what!

Bullbich I have a nose for these things and the closer I come to that fellow the more it starts to twitch. (*He sniffs*) There! He's here now. I can smell him.

Anton Well of course he's here. These are his headquarters. He's holding a council of war in the parlour. But if you can smell anything it must be Bobchinsky. He was here just now and there's a lingering smell of rotten fish wherever he goes. And as for you, you're just sulking because you've been made an exhibition of in the public streets. So now you want to get in touch with the Kremlin and blow everything sky high. Don't you understand that just a handful of men at the very top know what's happening here? And the commissar is their picked man? Why, he's done more for Poshlost in a week than we ever did in twenty years. The fellow's a miracle worker.

Bullbich But a bunch of lunatics!

Anton Would that we were so crazy, because they're miracle workers, too. Have you heard the latest? They stitched together all the straitwaistcoats and canvas strips from the asylum—you know, the canvas strips you were so fond of wetting and drying to make their eyes pop?—they've stitched them all together and made a conveyor belt. Why didn't you think of that? Now get out of here and supervise the traffic.

Bullbich But comrade——

Anton Be off with you!

Bullbich All right, but I'll remember this.

Anton Get out!

Bullbich leaves and slams the door

What have I done to be cursed with a blockhead like that for a son-in-law? He's as stubborn as that nogoodnik Sonya.

The door opens and Sonya enters followed by Osip. Sonya carries a soup tureen

Sonya (*sweetly*) His excellency the commissar. And the soup. (*She carries the soup to the table*)

Anton On your feet everybody!

Osip Please don't stand on ceremony. I'm only human, you know—underneath.

Anton Oh, the commissar is too modest. Please do us the honour of sitting down at our humble table.

They all sit

Anna Sonya, bring in the vegetables.

Sonya Yes, ma'am.

Sonya goes

Anna May I help your excellency to a little soup?

Osip (*hopefully*) Vegetable soup?

Anna examines the soup with a spoon

Anna Oh dear, it seems to be chicken noodle.

Osip Oh, no thank you. You know, I haven't tasted a vegetable since I came here. I don't half miss them.

Anna Vegetables are on the way.

Osip Oh, well, in that case I'll try a slice of beef.

Sonya enters with vegetable tureens on a tray or trolley

Natasha Can I give you a hand, Sonya?

Sonya Thank you, Natasha, I can manage.

Osip (*sniffing*) Good heavens, what's this? (*He raises a metal lid*) Oh, look at that, a mountain of fresh peas.

Anna Picked this morning, Osip Konstantinovich.

Osip raises another lid

Osip Oh—yum—beaded brawns! (*He raises another lid*) Oh, beautiful! Bartered pussnips. My favourite. You know something, I don't know where to start.

Sonya You don't start.

Osip I beg your pardon.

Sonya I said you don't start, comrade.

Anna Sonya! How dare you!

Sonya How could I let him eat the crops of speculation—grown with my own filthy hands in the valley of exploitation?

Anton Sonya! I'm warning you.

Sonya I couldn't be so unfair to him.

Osip Unfair?

Sonya One mouthful would make you a monopolist by association.

Osip But I'm practically a vegetarian. Look, I've hardly beefed with my toy.

Sonya Does anybody else want vegetables? (*Pause*) Then I'll clear them away.

Sonya wheels out the trolley of vegetables and closes the door behind her

Anton (*whispering*) Don't you fear, your excellency, I'll smuggle some of them to your room when she's out.

The door opens and Sonya's head appears

Sonya No you won't, Anton Antonovich. They're going straight into the pigswill.

Sonya disappears

Anna This is what comes of abolishing the serfs. Excuse me, comrade, I'll just have a word with her.

Anna exits

Anton I don't know how to apologize, comrade. What can one do with such a girl?

Osip Take her for a wife.

Anton (*aside*) Take away her life! My God, and he'll take mine if I'm not

careful. It's time I was gone. (*Aloud*) Excuse me, your excellency, it's time
I was clocking on at the tractor works. Good-night.

Anton exits

Natasha Don't be angry with her, comrade. She's just headstrong.
Osip Yes, I know, but she'll come round to my way of thinking.
Natasha You sound very sure of yourself.
Osip Yes, it's because I can do no wrong, you see.
Natasha I beg your pardon?
Osip I'm infallible. Comrade, can I confide in you? Ivan Alexandrovich said
I should if I had any problems.
Natasha Ivan Alexandrovich? Said you should confide in me?
Osip Yes, he said you were a twenty-four year old carrot.
Natasha He said what!
Osip Gold. Pure. Twenty-four carat.
Natasha (*happily*) He said that about me? (*Angrily*) Well who gives a hang
for his opinion?
Osip You only think of him as a bedfellow, don't you?
Natasha What!
Osip A bad fellow. But he's the best fellow I've ever met. And he told me to
come to you with my problems. Well, as I say, I seem to be infallible and
to be honest it's all quite worrying. My parents brought me up as a good
atheist but sometimes just lately I've had the funny feeling that I'm being
taken care of.
Natasha Who by? In what way?
Osip I lead a charmed life. For instance, you probably hadn't noticed but
sometimes my tongue plays tricks with me and I talk a lot of nonsense.
But it makes no difference. It even helps. The other day we were all sitting
round the table and wondering how we could get our hands on more
pressed steel and engine parts and I said, "Comrades, I'm wracking my
brains."
Natasha What's wrong with that?
Osip It came out as, "Comrades, try hijacking trains." And the comrades
took me at my word.
Natasha How do you mean?
Osip They went out and raided a train and now we've got enough raw
materials to run a dozen tractor factories. You might say that was just a
fluke, but then we had the problem of sobering up the workforce and the
Red Army gun platoon. They used to drive into town in their armoured
cars and requisition whatever they liked.
Natasha I know.
Osip Vodka mostly.
Natasha I'd noticed.
Osip Well, I saw nothing for it but to demobilize the artillery. But I was so
nervous about standing up to the army that you know what I said?
Natasha I can't wait?
Osip Immobilize the distillery.
Natasha (*laughing*) Immobilize the distillery!

Osip Yes, and the comrades went right out and dismantled it and everybody sobered up overnight—even the gunners. So do you understand?
I'm taken care of. And that's why Sonya Alexandrovna will see things my
way in the end. Today she won't give me a vegetable but tomorrow—you
see—she'll come to me with open arms and give me all the greens I want.

The Lights fade to a Black-out

SCENE 2

Among the beanrows in Sonya's private plot

Sonya is hoeing her beans and waving away bees

Sonya Buzz buzz buzz. Oh, buzz off, do, you silly old bee. Land on a bean
flower, not on me.

Natasha enters moonily

Good heavens, you've come to give me a hand.
Natasha Give you a hand?
Sonya Weeding these beans. The children are all back at school.
Natasha How can you talk about weeding beans when I've said yes to
Colonel Bullbich? I'm going to drown myself like Ophelia. I'm going to
throw myself under a train like Anna Karenina. I'm going to take arsenic
like Madame Bovary.
Sonya And you still call reading a healthy pastime?
Natasha Tomorrow I'm getting married to a creature I can't stand and just
because I wanted to spite a man who's probably forgotten my existence.
Yet I can't stand him either. Sonya, how can it be that we can long for
somebody when all our senses tell us they're rotten through and through?
Sonya What's the mystery? A bee comes along and deposits a bit of pollen
on you and you're a goner. Yes and there's been one buzzing around me
for days. There it is now. Go on! Get off with you!
Osip (*off*) Son-y-aa!
Natasha Oh, no, it's your dreadful commissar.
Sonya *My* commissar?
Natasha Yes, I don't want to see him. I'm going to sit in the birch
plantation and read Pushkin.

Natasha goes. Osip enters

Sonya ignores him and hoes furiously. He follows her up and down the row

Osip Sonya——
Sonya Oh, buzz off, will you, I'm busy.
Osip Aren't you forgetting what I am?
Sonya No, you're a thief.
Osip A thief?
Sonya My vegetables were pilfered during the night. Two cabbages and a
row of peas. Was it you? Yes, you've turned crimson.

Osip That's enough! I'm a commissar!

Sonya Take your hands off me!

Osip No. Keep still. I could have you shot.

Sonya Then why don't you?

Osip Because I—because I want to—when I look into your eyes I want to . . .

Sonya Yes?

Osip I want to reform you. By the way, those beans have got a nasty case of blossom drop. You should give them a good drenching as soon as the sun goes down, and then some liquid manure in the morning.

Sonya You see? You're not a commissar at heart. You're a gardener. Oh, Osip, you'd make such a wonderful farmer.

Osip A farmer? But I'm a ruler.

Sonya But rulers are ten to the copeck. Lose one ruler and ten new ones spring up like nettles. Lose one farmer and all Russia tightens its belt. One fills our head with lies and the other fills our bellies with food.

Osip (*sighing*) Oh, it's hopeless, isn't it? You're a confirmed capitalistic entrepreneur and I'm a pure Marxist Leninist and the two can never lie down together—I beg your pardon—jump into bed together—no—I mean——

Sonya Look! Somebody's coming.

Osip What? Oh, yes. No! It can't be. Good heavens, it is!

Ivan enters

Ivan Osip!

Osip Ivan Alexandrovich!

Ivan Osip the Terribly Great!

Osip Comrade!

Osip and Ivan embrace

Ivan My goodness, such medals! It's like embracing a Rolls Royce radiator.

Osip Comrade, there's so much to report.

Ivan Yes, but later, where's Natasha Antonovna?

Osip Everything unfolded as you said it would, comrade, only better.

Ivan Yes, that's marvellous, but where's Natasha?

Osip Poshlost is a new town.

Ivan Yes, I'm so happy for you, but where is——?

Osip We hijacked a drain—no, a train.

Sonya Be quiet! The man wants Natasha. She's up there in the birch grove, comrade. (*Calling*) Natasha! Natasha! (*Pause*) There's a visitor for you! (*Pause*) It's Ivan Alexandrovich!

Birds fly up in the trees

Come on, Osip.

Osip Now wait a minute. Ivan Alexandrovich wants to hear a full report.

Sonya No he doesn't. Come.

Osip You let go of me!

Sonya (*going*) We're not wanted here.

Osip Sonya—my arm—ooh—stop that—ow!

Sonya drags Osip off

Ivan (*to himself*) Ah, there she comes—out of the trees. See how she flies. Always remember this moment. A soft summer evening with a fine mist giving a feeling of the sea beyond the trees. And Natasha running to me down the hill.

Natasha arrives and stands some distance away

Natasha.

Natasha (*panting*) Well . . .

Ivan Won't you come closer?

Natasha I—I . . .

Ivan Come closer.

Natasha I—I don't want to.

Ivan Why not?

Natasha I hate you. I despise you.

Ivan Natasha.

Natasha No, stay where you are.

Ivan But darling.

Natasha I want to tear your eyes out. I want to boil you in oil. I want to bake your bread and have your babies.

Ivan Darling. Darling.

Natasha Kiss me. Kiss me.

Ivan (*kissing her*) Oh, Natasha, Natasha.

Natasha Vanya, Vanya. (*She breaks free*) No! What am I doing? Let me go.

Ivan But why?

Natasha Because you're a commissar and I—well .. .

Ivan What? You think I'm too grand for you?

Natasha Too grand? What nonsense! Don't you know I'm descended from the old nobility? Good heavens, one of my ancestors signed the declaration liberating the serfs.

Ivan Good heavens, one of mine signed the Ten Commandments.

Pause

Natasha What? I don't believe you.

Ivan It's the truth.

Natasha But since when did they start appointing Jewish commissars?

Ivan The moment I arrived in Poshlost. It was your father who decided we were commissars.

Natasha Then what are you?

Ivan I'm a poet. I was booked for the asylum. Thanks to your father I was given the chance to escape to the West, but I had to turn back.

Natasha Why?

Ivan Because a strange thing happens to your heart when you contemplate leaving Russia. This land isn't a KGB man with a hatchet face. It isn't a Red Army general in jackboots. It's a girl in a birch glade reading Pushkin. And I want to spend my life with her.

Natasha Ivan Alexandrovich, was that just a metaphor—or a proposal of marriage?
Ivan I'm asking you to marry me.
Natasha Darling, I'm already engaged.
Ivan Darling, so disengage.
Natasha Darling, I will!
Ivan Darling, I . . . but wait!
Natasha What is it?
Ivan There's somebody hiding behind that row of beans. Come out, whoever you are! (*Pause*) Osip!

Osip emerges from behind the beans

Osip Yes, comrade.
Ivan How long have you been there?
Osip Long enough, comrade.
Ivan Good. So I needn't explain.
Osip No, comrade, I recognize insanity when I see it.
Natasha But Osip, listen to me——
Ivan No, Natasha, leave this to me. You go home. I'll see you tomorrow at the Palace of Weddings.
Natasha The palace of . . . yes! (*Going*) I'll see you at the Palace of Weddings.

Natasha exits in a joyful dream

Pause

Ivan Osip, what can I say? I deceived you. I'm sorry.
Osip No, comrade, you've gone crazy and it's my duty as a commissar to put you away.
Ivan Osip, you're not a commissar.
Osip Of course I'm a commissar. Look at these medals.
Ivan Yes, you appear to be suffering from medalomania. But you're still not a commissar. You're a boy with a dog named Bobik.

Pause

Osip You tricked me. You fooled me. You let me walk up and down this town clanking with medals. You made me do all this mischief.
Ivan But it wasn't like that at all! Wait. What do you mean—mischief?
Osip The terrible things I've done to this little town.
Ivan Terrible? But you've done wonders. Poshlost is a new town. Ten minutes ago you were boasting about it. Why is it suddenly so terrible?
Osip Why? Why? Because we haven't got the blessing of the Kremlin. Because we've acted like irresponsible hooligans.
Ivan Oy-oy-oy! We kicked the irresponsible hooligans out, remember? And hasn't it worked?
Osip Maybe it has, but it isn't Communism.
Ivan But surely it matters not if the cat is white or black as long as it catches mice.
Osip It matters if it isn't a Communist cat.

Ivan Such a cat hasn't been seen in this country since the death of Lenin.
Listen, when I got off the train just now and saw Lenin's statue gleaming
in Gorky Square, the two names suddenly swam together—Lenin and
Gorky. And I remembered how the Tzar exiled Gorky to a sleepy little
town in Southern Russia because of his revolutionary activities. And it
came to me what Lenin said about that: "One of Europe's foremost
writers, whose only weapon is free speech, is being banished by the
autocratic government without trial." And as I passed by I said, "You
cried out in vain, brother, because it's still going on, only worse. But not
in Poshlost."

Osip All right! Prince Lucifer can quote the Communist Manifesto but I
don't have to listen. Poshlost is going back on a proper Soviet footing.

Ivan What do you mean by that?

Osip To the way it was before.

Ivan What? Your thirty-four comrades flung back in the madhouse?

Osip If the state says that's where they belong.

Ivan Do you say so?

Osip Why not? They're criminals.

Ivan Are you sure of that? I thought they were your friends.

Osip Friends or not, they're public enemies!

Ivan Do you really believe that?

Osip Just shut up! Stop trying to trick me! I may have been a fool but I still
know my duty.

Ivan Oh, Osip, Osip!

Osip I said shut up! I'm going to put things right here. I'll put the tractor
factory in production. I'll flood this valley. Then I'll make my confession
and take my medicine.

Ivan And all Poshlost will take its medicine. They'll wipe it off the map
because freedom and justice were once known here. On the other hand,
Osip, if we can keep up the pretence long enough, all Russia might learn
from its example. It takes only one little stone to start an avalanche.

Osip You mean one bad apple to rot all the rest. Well, the rot stops here!
(*Laughing*) Osip the Terribly Great! What a joke! Osip the Amazing
Chump, that's me. And the strange thing is I knew all the time I wasn't a
commissar. How could I be? I couldn't even grow a moustache. But I let
myself be led on. It was these medals. This uniform. The cult of
personality. Napoleonic self-aggrandizement. I let myself have crazy
dreams. I was going to walk up and down Moscow all dressed to kill with
Mother on one arm and Tatiana on the other, and Bobik trotting behind
on a new leather lead. But it was all your big joke. Oh, comrade, I thought
so much of you. I was going to take you home to meet Tatiana, that's how
much I thought of you. And all the time you were laughing at me. That's
what I can't forgive. Well, there's only one thing to do in a case like this.
You'll have to give me satisfaction, comrade, that's all.

Ivan Satisfaction?

Osip Yes.

Ivan But surely you don't mean . . . ?

Osip Yes, I believe the choice of weapons is yours.

Ivan A duel? Are you crazy?

Osip Are you a coward?

Ivan Of course I'm a coward.

Osip If you live you can run Poshlost your way. If not I'll put it back on a proper Soviet footing. Now will you fight?

Pause

Ivan For that, I have to fight.

Osip Name the weapons.

Ivan What's the difference? Pistols, I suppose.

Osip Have you ever fired one?

Ivan Good heavens, no.

Osip I must warn you, comrade, I was a crack shot in the Komsomol pistol team.

Ivan Ah. I'll just have to pin my hopes on beginner's luck.

Osip What if I make a hole in you?

Ivan That's an occupational risk for a poet in this country. The moment we lift a pen somebody cocks a pistol.

Osip When shall we meet?

Ivan Isn't dawn a popular hour for these amusements?

Osip Very well, dawn. You'd better go and find a second.

Ivan Yes, of course. Until dawn then.

Osip Good-night, comrade.

Ivan (*going*) Good-night, Osip.

Ivan exits. As he does so he passes Sonya, entering

Sonya (*to Ivan*) Hello, comrade. (*To Osip*) What's the matter with him? He didn't even speak to me.

Osip He's going to be buried.

Sonya Buried? You mean married? To Natasha? I knew it! So that's why he was looking so pale. Married. What right have they to do a thing like that in a world like this? But they're so weak. Nature strikes and they're powerless to resist. But it won't catch me so easily. (*Pause*) Now what did I come back for? Oh yes.

Osip Oh what?

Sonya No—hoe. H—O—E.

Osip Ah. I mean oh. I mean——

Sonya Never mind. Here it is.

Osip Ah. I mean——

Sonya Oh, shut up, will you. (*Pause*) What are you staring at?

Osip You've let your hair down. It's beautiful.

Sonya Yes, it's wet. I want it to dry. I've been for a swim.

Osip Oh? Where?

Sonya In the next valley.

Osip Oh? Is there a pool?

Sonya A pool? It's all awash. That's what I keep trying to tell you.

Osip Pardon?

Sonya There's a sea. That's where we diverted the river Posh from this valley.

Osip What? You what? You mean there's a Posh, all awash, in the vast nelly?

Sonya Damn it, Osip, the next valley!

Osip Dam it? You mean I could? It could be? It would?

Sonya Calm down!

Osip So this one needn't be floundered? And then you'd let me have you?

Sonya I beg your pardon?

Osip Let me have it. Let me drown you. In holy water. Hemlock. Wedlock.

Pause

Sonya Osip Konstantinovich, are you asking me to marry you?

Osip Yes, I am, Sonya Alexandrovna.

Sonya And you won't flood my valley?

Osip Of course not. And not only that. Everything's going to be the same as it was before.

Sonya Good. Wait. What do you mean by that exactly?

Osip Poshlost. It's going back on a proper Soviet footing. It'll be just like it was before we arrived.

Sonya What? You mean a crooked vodka-swilling shambles?

Osip What? Er, well . . .

Sonya Tell me you're joking.

Osip Well . . .

Sonya But you must be! Look at it now—spread out in the sunset. All is peace in Poshlost. They've mended the hole in the cathedral dome. All the good books are back on the library shelves. There's no bribery or drunkenness or cheating any more. And all because of you. They say we might produce our first tractor tomorrow. I've got my name down for it. Natasha Antonovna and Ivan Alexandrovich are going to be married. We're going to be married.

Osip We are?

Sonya Yes. Our children and theirs will grow up side by side in this little town and one day they might marry and have their own beautiful tractors.

Osip Yes, I see it! I see it! (*Pause*) But wait. Oh, no.

Sonya Is something wrong?

Osip I was forgetting.

Sonya Oh?

Osip Ivan Alexandrovich.

Sonya What about him?

Osip We've a meeting tomorrow.

Sonya What time tomorrow?

Osip Very early. Dawn.

Sonya Well, we've all the rest of the day to marry in. Don't pull such a face.

Osip Could you leave me alone for a while? I must write to my parents. Just in case.

Sonya In case of what?

Osip Just to warn them.
Sonya About us?
Osip What's that? Oh, yes.
Sonya You make it sound like a funeral. All right, I'll leave you alone. Give
    them my love and a million kisses. I'll say good-night. Don't stay out too
    late. (*Going*) Until tomorrow then—at the Palace of Weddings.

Sonya goes

Pause

Osip (*alone*) A million kisses . . . and she never gave me one. Maybe she
    never will. I could withdraw. What is there to fight about? But no, he
    insulted me. God, what a muddle.

The Lights fade to a Black-out

SCENE 3

Anton's house

Ivan is alone writing a letter. There is a knock on the door

Sonya enters

Sonya Ivan Alexandrovich.
Ivan Yes, Sonya?
Sonya Trouble.
Ivan Oh?
Sonya It's Colonel Bullbich. He insists on seeing you.
Ivan I thought he might. Very well, send him in. Hold on a minute, though.
    It's past midnight. Why aren't you in bed?
Sonya I'm sewing my wedding dress.
Ivan I see. Wear it in good health, Sonya. All right, send him in.
Sonya Be careful. He has a big pistol.

Sonya exits; Bullbich enters

Ivan Come in, Colonel.
Bullbich Natasha Antonovna has just returned my ring.
Ivan Yes, I thought she might.
Bullbich Seven hundred roubles—from Budapest!
Ivan Some you win, some you lose.
Bullbich Let me just say this: you might be a commissar and you might not.
    But you leave me no choice.
Ivan Don't tell me. You demand satisfaction?
Bullbich Naturally.
Ivan Pistols?
Bullbich Splendid.
Ivan At dawn?
Bullbich I'll be at your disposal.

Ivan Dawn is a trifle inconvenient. I have a previous engagement. Could we say half an hour later?
Bullbich As you wish. Good-night.

Bullbich exits, only to return immediately

Incidentally, in the meantime, I'm going to telegraph Moscow and question your status here.
Ivan Ah.
Bullbich Good-night.

Bullbich exits

Ivan Oy-oy-oy!

The Lights fade to a Black-out

SCENE 4

A birch glade

Osip and Dobchinsky are present but hidden behind a tree

Bobchinsky enters, leading Ivan

Bobchinsky This way, comrade, just follow me.
Ivan Bobchinsky, are you sure you know where we're going?
Bobchinsky Oh yes. (*He sniffs the air*) That's very peculiar. Can you smell anything?
Ivan Fish.
Bobchinsky That's quite right. A distinct smell of fish. I wonder where it could be coming from.
Ivan Yes, but hadn't we better press on? The dawn's breaking.
Bobchinsky One moment. (*He starts turning out his pockets*)
Ivan Oy! What are you doing?
Bobchinsky Good heavens! (*He finds something in his back pocket*)
Ivan What's the matter?
Bobchinsky Have you had breakfast, comrade?
Ivan Of course not.
Bobchinsky You don't happen to fancy a pickled herring?
Ivan No. Now come on.
Bobchinsky Yes.

Pause, then Osip and Dobchinsky come out of hiding

Ah, your opponent's already arrived, you see? Yes and there's Dobchinsky with the pistols.
Ivan Bobchinsky, are you sure nobody knows about this? We won't be disturbed?
Bobchinsky Oh, it's completely confidential. Take my word.
Ivan Right. Let's get it over.
Bobchinsky Dobchinsky!

Dobchinsky Bobchinsky!

Bobchinsky Osip Konstantinovich! Good-morning!

Osip Oh, good-morning.

Bobchinsky You don't happen to be feeling a little peckish, do you, because I happen to have on me——

Ivan That will do, Bobchinsky! Hello, Osip.

Osip Good-morning, comrade.

Bobchinsky Gentlemen, Dobchinsky and I must discuss the arrangements for a moment in private. Perhaps in the meantime you could be selecting your weapons. Dobchinsky, come over here for a moment.

Bobchinsky and Dobchinsky go into a confidential huddle

Dobchinsky Yes, what is it?

Bobchinsky You didn't tell anybody about this, did you?

Dobchinsky Not a soul, on my honour, except the postman.

Bobchinsky Neither did I. Apart from the barber.

Dobchinsky Yes and the result is——

Bobchinsky Every tree in this birch glade has somebody behind it.

Dobchinsky And somebody up it.

Bobchinsky Yes, in fact everyone in town is present.

Dobchinsky Except the night shift of the tractor factory.

Bobchinsky You mean Anton Antonovich is absent?

Dobchinsky He's supervising the night shift. Oh, and his wife isn't here. She fell asleep sewing bridal gowns.

Bobchinsky What about the two brides?

Dobchinsky Sleeping. It would have been a shame to spoil their wedding eve.

Bobchinsky But otherwise it's a splendid turnout.

Dobchinsky Capital. We've seen nothing like this since the Dynamos played Poshlost Wanderers.

Bobchinsky Very well, we'd better begin. Gentlemen! Are you ready? Splendid. Now this engagement will be fought according to the classic French code. Dobchinsky has marked out a line——

Dobchinsky Forty-two paces long.

Bobchinsky Dobchinsky, please, allow me! In the centre there is a no-man's-land, ten paces long. You will take up your positions at either end of the line——

Dobchinsky Facing each other.

Bobchinsky Facing each other, of course. Dobchinsky, do you mind? You will face each other and keep the muzzles of your pistols pointing to the ground. At a given signal——

Dobchinsky The raising and dropping of his handkerchief.

Bobchinsky The raising and dropping of my handkerchief, you will advance on each other. You may fire whenever you think proper. Now if one of you fires and misses, the other can wait until his opponent has advanced right up to the barrier——

Dobchinsky And take a long cool aim.

Bobchinsky Yes. Very well, gentlemen, take up your positions please.

They do

Thank you. That will do.

Ivan Hold it, Bobchinsky, a word with you, please. Over here.

Bobchinsky (*going to Ivan; whispering*) Well, comrade?

Ivan Have you a light?

Bobchinsky You want a cigarette?

Ivan No, I want to light this candle and put melted wax in my ears. I'm scared of loud bangs.

Bobchinsky Really? (*He strikes a match*) There you are, comrade. Tell me, what are your tactics?

Ivan I'm going to walk straight up to the barrier and if he hasn't sent me to heaven by then I'll do my best to put a little red badge between his eyes.

Bobchinsky Good heavens, is that the only way you can make sure of hitting him?

Ivan On the contrary. It's the only way I can make sure of missing him.

Bobchinsky and Ivan move away. Pause

Osip Dobchinsky! Psst! Dobchinsky!

Dobchinsky Yes, comrade?

Osip Over here. Quick.

Dobchinsky goes to Osip

Dobchinsky (*whispering*) Yes, Osip Konstantinovich?

Osip You didn't give me my ear-plugs.

Dobchinsky Oh, sorry, I forgot.

Osip The sound of a pistol gives me a headache.

Dobchinsky Here they are comrade.

Osip Thank you.

Dobchinsky Oh, look at poor Ivan Alexandrovich. Lighting a candle. Fancy, offering up a prayer.

Osip He needn't worry.

Dobchinsky What do you mean, comrade?

Osip I'm going to walk up to the barrier without firing. If he hasn't killed me by then I'll just close my eyes and fire to one side. So keep well clear.

Dobchinsky But comrade.

Osip I can't hear you. Just do as I say.

Bobchinsky (*calling*) Well, Dobchinsky, is your man ready?

Dobchinsky Ready, Bobchinsky.

Bobchinsky Very well. Then I'll give the signal.

Dobchinsky Wait! There's somebody coming!

Natasha (*together,* Vanya! Ivan! You can't do this to each other!
Sonya *off*) Osip! Stop this nonsense at once!

Dobchinsky Two girls dressed in white.

Bobchinsky Good lord, with bunches of flowers.

Dobchinsky It can't be.

Bobchinsky But it is.

Dobchinsky The two brides.

Natasha and Sonya rush on

Natasha Ivan!
Sonya Osip!
Dobchinsky (*restraining Natasha and Sonya*) I'm sorry, ladies, they're deaf
to all entreaties. Very well, my dear Bobchinsky, what are you waiting
for? Give the signal.
Bobchinsky Eh? Oh yes, right you are. (*He raises his right arm dramatically,
pauses, then drops it*)

Ivan and Osip march towards each other

> *They have gone only a few steps when Bullbich, out of their vision, appears
> at the back of the stage. He is accompanied by a richly-uniformed,
> jackbooted army general*

Bullbich Halt! Halt, I say, in the name of the party.

Ivan and Osip, being deaf, keep going

Attention! This is the commissar from Moscow! Who has come here to
... I said HALT! You men with the pistols! Stop! Stop!

*Ivan and Osip reach the barrier and face each other from a close distance.
They raise their pistols and aim one at the other. Then, still staring at each
other, they turn their pistols aside and fire. Bullbich and the Commissar fall.
The hidden crowd cheers and applauds*

Bobchinsky My goodness, did you see that? They both missed.
Dobchinsky But of course they didn't miss.
Bobchinsky (*seeing the bodies*) Oh, no, Dobchinsky.
Dobchinsky Oh, yes, Bobchinsky.
Bobchinsky Just listen to the crowd.
Dobchinsky A standing ovation.

*Ivan hands his pistol to Bobchinsky, who hands it to Dobchinsky, who hands it
back to Bobchinsky, who hands it back to Dobchinsky, who finally hands it to
Osip, who now has a pistol in each hand. An approaching engine is heard. All
look up in the air, except Dobchinsky, who looks left*

Bobchinsky (*dodging about*) Planes! Aeroplanes! We're under attack!
All but Dobchinsky Where? Where is it?
Dobchinsky No, no, no, it's not up there. It's down here. (*Pointing*) Look,
coming through the trees.
Bobchinsky Where? My God! What on earth is that?
Dobchinsky There, it's stopped. A tree in the way.
Sonya Natasha, am I dreaming or do you see what I see?
Natasha What do you see?
Sonya A brand new tractor—bright red—with a big blue bow on the
bonnet.
Natasha And my father in the driving seat and Mamushka at his side in all
her wedding finery. They're getting down. (*Opening her arms*) Father!

Anton enters in greasy overalls and a shiny topper and embraces Natasha.
He is followed by Anna, dressed to devastate

Anton My little Natushka! Blessings, my darling, on your wedding day. But
I have an announcement. My friends—I don't know how to say this—I
am so overcome—but my dear friends—my loved ones—I am honoured
to announce—Poshlost has produced her first tractor!

Anton is cheered and congratulated and slapped on the back, Sonya jumps up
and down in delight

Sonya Poshlost has produced a tractor! Poshlost has produced a tractor!
(*Heading off*) I'm first on the list!
Osip Stop! Silence! Sonya, come back here.

Sonya comes meekly to Osip's side. He hands one pistol to Bobchinsky and the
other to Dobchinsky

And now there's something I must do. (*He takes the Order of Lenin from*
his pocket and addresses Anton) Comrades, in the name of the people,
permit me to restore this medal to its plateful of rice.

All eyes turn to Sonya for the translation

Sonya Its rightful place.

Osip pins the medal on Anton. Everybody cheers and claps, including Anton

Anton And now come, everybody. Our conveyance is waiting. All aboard
our glorious tractor. All of you.
All All of us?
Anton Yes, all aboard! She's a true Russian tractor and not one of your
tinpot Western models.
Natasha But Father, where are we going?
Anna Where do you think, my darlings! To the Palace of Weddings.
Anton No, no confound it! To the cathedral!

Sonya rushes off to the tractor, closely followed by Anton, dragging Anna
behind him

Ivan lifts Natasha in his arms and carries her off

Osip stands staring to the front in a daze. Behind his back, Bobchinsky and
Dobchinsky go up to the bodies and place one pistol in the hand of Bullbich and
one in the hand of the Commissar

Bobchinsky and Dobchinsky then shake hands and tiptoe off, leaving Osip
alone

Sonya rushes back, lifts Osip in her arms and carries him off

The Lights fade to a Black-out

CURTAIN

FURNITURE AND PROPERTY LIST

ACT I

SCENE 1

On stage: Bench
Statue of Lenin
Timetable
Trestle-table. *On it:* rubber stamps, passport documents, tickets, etc.

Off stage: Baggage for two **(Sonya)**
Rucksack **(Ivan)**
Expensive luggage containing denims etc. **(Anton** and **Anya)**

Personal: **Sergeant:** revolver
Ivan: handkerchief
Osip: handkerchief

SCENE 2

On stage: All luggage, including a pigskin portmanteau
Trolley

SCENE 3

On stage: Overstuffed chairs
Lamps with silk-tasselled shades
Portrait of Lenin
Drinks table. *On it:* bottles and glasses
Table. *On it:* paper, pens etc.
Chair

Off stage: Damaged bunch of roses **(Bullbich)**

Personal: **Bullbich:** scrap of paper
Anton: roubles

SCENE 4

On stage: Nil

SCENE 5

On stage: Overstuffed chairs
Lamps with silk-tasselled shades
Portrait of Lenin

Drinks table. *On it:* bottles and glasses
Table. *On it:* paper, pens etc.
Chair

SCENE 6

On stage: Podium strung with bunting

Personal: **Natasha:** book of poetry
Bullbich: gold locket

ACT II

SCENE 1

On stage: Table. *On it:* bowls, plates, knives, forks, spoons
Chairs

Off stage: Soup tureen **(Sonya)**
Vegetable tureens on a tray or trolley **(Sonya)**

SCENE 2

On stage: Rows of beans
Hoe for **Sonya**

SCENE 3

On stage: Overstuffed chairs
Lamps with silk-tasselled shades
Portrait of Lenin
Drinks table. *On it:* bottles and glasses
Table. *On it:* paper, pens etc.
Chair

SCENE 4

On stage: Trees

Off stage: Bunches of flowers **(Natasha** and **Sonya)**

Personal: **Bobchinsky:** pickled herring, handkerchief and matches in pocket
Dobchinsky: pistols, ear-plugs
Ivan: candle
Osip: Order of Lenin

LIGHTING PLOT

ACT I, Scene 1

To open: General exterior lighting, summer

Cue 1   **Sergeant:** "Oh well, Siberia can sleep in peace."   (Page 12)
         Fade to black-out

ACT I, Scene 2

To open: General exterior lighting, summer

Cue 2   **Anton, Anna** and **Dobchinsky** exit   (Page 18)
         Fade to black-out

ACT I, Scene 3

To open: General interior lighting

Cue 3   **Ivan:** "In here! At the double!"   (Page 24)
         Fade to black-out

ACT I, Scene 4

To open: Exterior, just before sunset, summer

Cue 4   **Osip:** "Commissar?"   (Page 26)
         Fade to black-out

ACT I, Scene 5

To open: General interior lighting

Cue 5   **Ivan:** "In the madhouse."   (Page 28)
         Fade to black-out

ACT I, Scene 6

To open: General exterior lighting

Cue 6   **Bullbich:** "Here, let me put it round your pretty neck."   (Page 32)
         Fade to black-out

ACT II, Scene 1

To open: General interior lighting

Cue 7   **Osip:** "... give me all the greens I want."   (Page 37)
         Fade to black-out

ACT II, Scene 2

To open: General exterior, afternoon

Cue 8	When ready and then through scene	(Page 40)
	Gradually fade light as sunset approaches	
Cue 9	**Osip:** "God, what a muddle."	(Page 44)
	Fade to black-out	

ACT II, Scene 3

To open: Interior lighting, night, lamps lit

Cue 10	**Ivan:** "Oy-oy-oy!"	(Page 45)
	Fade to black-out	

ACT II, Scene 4

To open: Exterior, birch glade, early morning

Cue 11	When ready and then through scene	(Page 45)
	Bring up lights as dawn breaks	
Cue 12	**Sonya** lifts **Osip** in her arms and carries him off	(Page 49)
	Fade to black-out	

EFFECTS PLOT

In addition to the cues shown music could be used to accompany the scene changes—
see Production Note.

ACT I

ACT II

MADE AND PRINTED IN GREAT BRITAIN BY
LATIMER TREND & COMPANY LTD PLYMOUTH
MADE IN ENGLAND